Britain's
First Warplanes

Britain's First Warplanes

J. M. BRUCE

ARMS AND ARMOUR PRESS

First published in Great Britain
in 1987 by Arms and Armour Press Limited, Link House,
West Street, Poole, Dorset BH15 1LL.

Distributed in the USA by Sterling Publishing Co. Inc.,
2 Park Avenue, New York, NY 10016.

Distributed in Australia by
Capricorn Link (Australia) Pty. Ltd., P.O. Box 665,
Lane Cove, New South Wales 2066.

British Library Cataloguing in Publication data:
Bruce, J. M.
Britain's first warplanes.
1. Airplanes, Military—Great Britain—
History
I. Title
623.74'6'0941   UG1245.G7

ISBN 0-85368-852-4

The illustrations in this book have been collected from many
sources, and vary in quality owing to the variety of circumstances
in which they were taken and preserved. As a result, certain
of the illustrations are not of the standard to be expected from
the best of today's equipment, materials and techniques.

Edited and designed by Roger Chesneau; typeset by Typesetters
(Birmingham) Ltd; printed and bound in Great Britain.

They bear, in place of classic names,
Letters and numbers on their skin.

The Trade, Rudyard Kipling

Introduction

The Royal Flying Corps came into being on 13 April 1912, consisting essentially of a Naval Wing, a Military Wing, and a Central Flying School which was intended to train pilots for the operational Wings. The new service inherited an assortment of aircraft that had been acquired by the Air Battalion of the Royal Engineers and (reluctantly) by the Admiralty for the use of Naval aviators at Eastchurch. The Admiralty's acquisitions included some of the aircraft generously made available by Frank McClean, without whose vision and patriotism Naval aviation would have been very late in literally getting off the ground.

McClean owned a sizable personal fleet of aeroplanes, and had sensibly given them numerical identities in a straightforward series. When the War Office and Admiralty numbered their earliest aircraft, both decided to apply prefix letters to numerals. The Air Battalion's aeroplanes had either 'F' or 'B' as prefixes: 'F' derived from Farman and denoted pusher aircraft, whilst 'B' came from Blériot and was applied to tractor aircraft (this was continued in the 'FE' and 'BE' designations of the series of aircraft designed at the Royal Aircraft Factory, Farnborough). The Navy used three prefixes: 'H' for hydroplanes, 'M' for monoplanes and 'T' for tractors (presumably for biplanes and multiplanes).

The inconsistencies and complications of such refinements in numbering may seem obvious now, but at the time the reasons for their adoption must have been thought to be of some substance. A few months after the formation of the Royal Flying Corps both the Naval and Military series were superseded by a single simple numerical system in which, initially, the numbers 1–200 were allotted to the Naval Wing, 201–400 to the Military Wing and 401–600 to the Central Flying School.

Despite this basic rationalization, the allocations of serial numbers did not thereafter flow in consecutive sequence, most notably in the Military Wing, which decided to allot 201–250 for aircraft of No. 2 Squadron, 251–300 to No. 3 Squadron, 301–350 to No. 4 Squadron and 351–400 to No. 5 Squadron. This was intended to provide quick identification of the unit to which an aircraft belonged, but apparently was not scrupulously adhered to, and was abandoned when the allocation of numbers was taken over by the Aeronautical Inspection Department on 10 March 1914.

The Naval Wing allotted its numbers more or less in sequence as occasion required, but did not always hasten to paint them on the aircraft. By no means all of the first Naval 200 were taken up: it seems that some thirty aircraft were never delivered or not accepted.

In this book an attempt is made to illustrate as many as possible of the individual aircraft that were allotted the numbers from 1 to 400: these, with few exceptions, constituted the potentially operational aircraft of the two Wings. The notes that accompany the photographs give brief histories of the aircraft, in most cases greatly compressed. Several of these early military aircraft did indeed have modest operational careers in the war that broke out in August 1914, and a few distinguished themselves. Some survived into 1916, though how much of their original structure was still present then can only be conjectured; perhaps only the numbers survived.

By the time numbered Military and Naval aircraft were being seen with fair frequency, some civilian-owned aeroplanes were also wearing numbers. In

Officers of the Royal Naval Air Service at Hilsea at the time of the Royal Review of the Fleet, July 1914. At left is FSL C. Draper; fourth, fifth and sixth from left are, respectively, Cdr. C. R. Samson, Lt. R. L. G. Marix and Capt. I. T. Courtney RMLI. The aircraft is a Bristol T.B.8, either No. 43 or No. 153.

Officers of No. 2 Squadron, RFC (Military Wing), August 1913. From left to right: Capt. C. A. H. Longcroft, Capt. G. W. P. Dawes, Maj. J. H. W. Becke, Lt. F. F. Waldron, Lt. A. C. H. MacLean, Capt. F. St. G. Tucker and Lt. L. Dawes. Behind them is one of the squadron's B.E.2as. (RAF Museum)

the prewar period there was no registration system for such aircraft, and in the races that grew in popularity as public spectacles it became necessary for entrants to carry distinguishing numbers. Additionally, at Hendon some of the many aircraft using that popular aerodrome had local numbers: for example, the second Grahame-White single-rudder boxkite was No. 109 at Hendon and was reported as such as early as July 1913. Occasionally these non-RFC numbers have been misinterpreted, and confusion and misunderstandings have arisen.

Conversely, a few of these early Naval and Military aircraft never wore the serial numbers allotted to them, and, clearly, these can only be illustrated as they were (i.e. unmarked). Photographs of identifiable aircraft taken *before* their numbers were applied are also included; only in one or two cases does some doubt linger.

Contributions to the contents of this compilation have been made by many friends. To all who have made such a contribution I gratefully acknowledge my indebtedness, to none more than Stuart Leslie for his never-flagging efforts and unfailing support.

My thanks also go to Gordon Bruce; Graham Mottram and Len Lovell of the Fleet Air Arm Museum; Philip Jarrett; Peter Liddle, for the use of photographs from his 1914–18 Personal Experience Archives; Tim Mason; Ken Molson; Brian Kervell of the RAE Museum; Rick Barker and Reg Mack of the RAF Museum; Tom Goyer and Derek Jones of Short Brothers plc; Peter Wright; and to all who, over the years, have shared their photographic and documentary 'finds' with me and provided some of the facts and photographs reproduced herein. Photographs credited 'JMB/GSL' are from the J. M. Bruce/G. S. Leslie Collection.

Published 75 years after the formation of the Royal Flying Corps, this collection of photographs and notes has been assembled in the hope that it may serve both as a commemorative compilation and as a work of reference – a record of the beginnings of military aviation in Great Britain and a reminder of the debt we owe to the men whose names appear in these pages.

J. M. Bruce

LIST OF ABBREVIATIONS

AID	Aeronautical Inspection Department
B.E.	Blériot Experimental
Cdr.	Commander
CFS	Central Flying School
COW	Coventry Ordnance Works
DFW	Deutsche Flugzeug Werke
Eng. Lt.	Engineer Lieutenant
FAA	Fleet Air Arm
F.E.	Farman Experimental
FSL	Flight Sub-Lieutenant
HQ	Headquarters
H.R.E.	Hydroplane Reconnaissance Experimental
KAHRS	Kent Aviation and Historical Research Society
NAG	Neue Automobil Gesellschaft
NFS	Naval Flying School (previously Naval Aviation School)
PFSL	Probationary Flight Sub-Lieutenant
PRO	Public Record Office
RAE	Royal Aircraft Establishment
RAF	Royal Aircraft Factory
R.E.	Reconnaissance Experimental
RFC	Royal Flying Corps
RMA	Royal Marines Artillery
RMLI	Royal Marines Light Infantry
RN	Royal Navy
RNAS	Royal Naval Air Service
Salmson	Salmson (Système Canton-Unné). These aero-engines were frequently named simply Canton-Unné in official documents of the period.
SPA	Società Ligure Piemontese Automobili

Aircraft of the Naval Wing

A remarkable photograph of some of the RNAS seaplanes that were at Calshot in July 1914 to participate in the Royal Review of the Fleet. Those along the water's edge are (from left) Short Seaplanes, Admiralty Type 74, Nos. 75 and 74; Sopwith Bat-Boat No. 118 (with headlight mounted on the bows); Short Seaplanes Type 74, Nos. 76 and 77; and three Maurice Farman Seaplanes. At the rear, by the flagpole, stands the Sopwith Seaplane No. 151. (FAA Museum)

1 SHORT BIPLANE
S.34, ex-T1, 50hp Gnome (reconstructed as S.86 with 70hp Gnome)

This Sommer-type biplane was, in 1911, No. 6 of Frank McClean's fleet of aircraft and was one of those that he made available for the training of Naval pilots. Here (right, top) it is seen leaving Margate on 30 May 1912, piloted by Lt. C. J. L'Estrange Malone RN. Officially numbered T1 in 1912, it became No. 1 in the plain-number series. By December 1913 it had been reconstructed to the (production) Type S.38 configuration seen in the photograph at far right, and with the new Shorts number S.86. It gave long service at Eastchurch, latterly with a 70hp Gnome engine,

and was repeatedly damaged and repaired. A major modification to No. 1 was the fitting of a float undercarriage in March 1914 (right, below). In this form the aircraft was employed to test a version of the GRW Wheel Attachment (from the surname initials of its joint creators, Lt.Cdr. R. Gregory, Eng. Lt. E. W. Riley of HMS *Hermes* and Mr. White of Chatham Dockyard), but later reverted to having a conventional wheel undercarriage. It was finally deleted on 22 February 1916 (JMB/GSL; Shorts; PRO: AIR 2/164/MR 10721)

2 SHORT BIPLANE
S.38, ex-T2, 50hp Gnome (later 70hp Gnome)

As first completed, the Short S.38 was similar to the original form of S.34, and was used at the Royal Naval Aviation School at Eastchurch. With flotation gear fitted, as seen here, it was successfully put down on the Medway by Lt. A. M. Longmore RN

on 1 December 1911; on 10 January 1912 Lt. C. R. Samson RN flew it from a platform on HMS *Africa*; and on 9 May 1912 Samson took off from HMS *Hibernia* while the ship was under way. By June 1912 the S.38 had the identity T2. (Philip M. Jarrett)

2 SHORT PUSHER BIPLANE
S.38 rebuilt, 70hp Gnome

The original S.38 was wrecked on 9 July 1912 while being hoisted aboard HMS *London*, but, 'converted into late Farman style and weighing rather less than before', it was flying again on 29 August. On 7 September 1912 Lt. W. Parke RN made one of the earliest night flights on this aircraft. The photograph on the right was taken at Eastchurch on 10 October 1912, when No. 2 was being flown by Lt. C. J. L'Estrange Malone RN, with Lt. R. H. Clark Hall RN as passenger. No. 2 was much used as a trainer at Eastchurch, and on 1 February 1913 a further reconstruction began. This continued at least until 29 March and the aircraft resumed its training activities, which brought further repairs and reconstructions. By September 1914, when the photograph below was taken with FSL J. P. Wilson aboard, the nacelle shape had been altered, a new and stronger undercarriage had been fitted and the fuel tank had been mounted in a lower position. No. 2's flying career ended in a crash on 28 January 1915, and it was deleted on 20 February that year. (Philip M. Jarrett; Peter Liddle)

3 SHORT TRIPLE-TWIN BIPLANE
S.39, ex-T3, 2×50hp Gnome

The first aircraft associated with the original number T3 was the Short Triple-Twin, which had two 50hp Gnome engines driving three propellers. It first flew on 18 September 1911, piloted by its owner, Frank McClean, in whose stable it was No. 10. Naval pilots who flew it included Lts. A. M. Longmore, R. Gregory and C. J. L'Estrange Malone. By mid-June 1912 it had been marked 'T3'. (JMB/GSL)

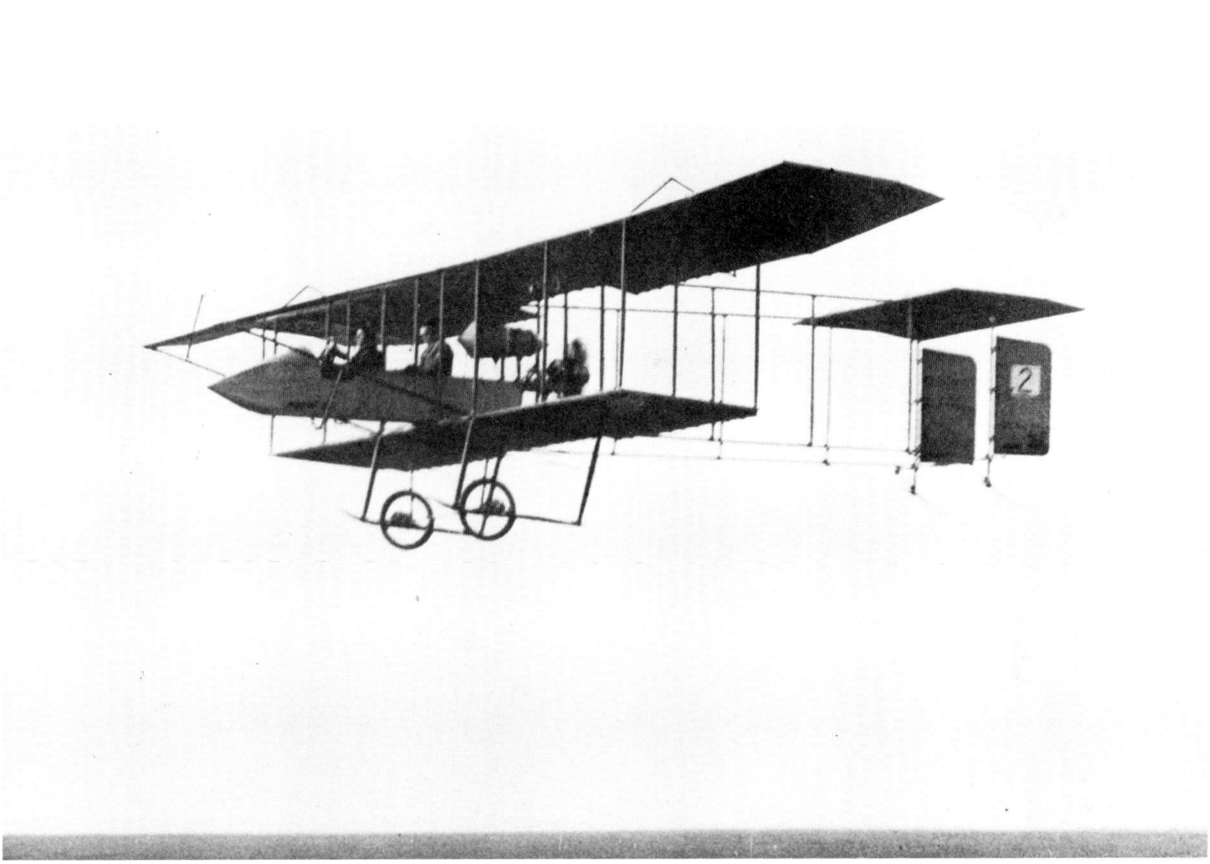

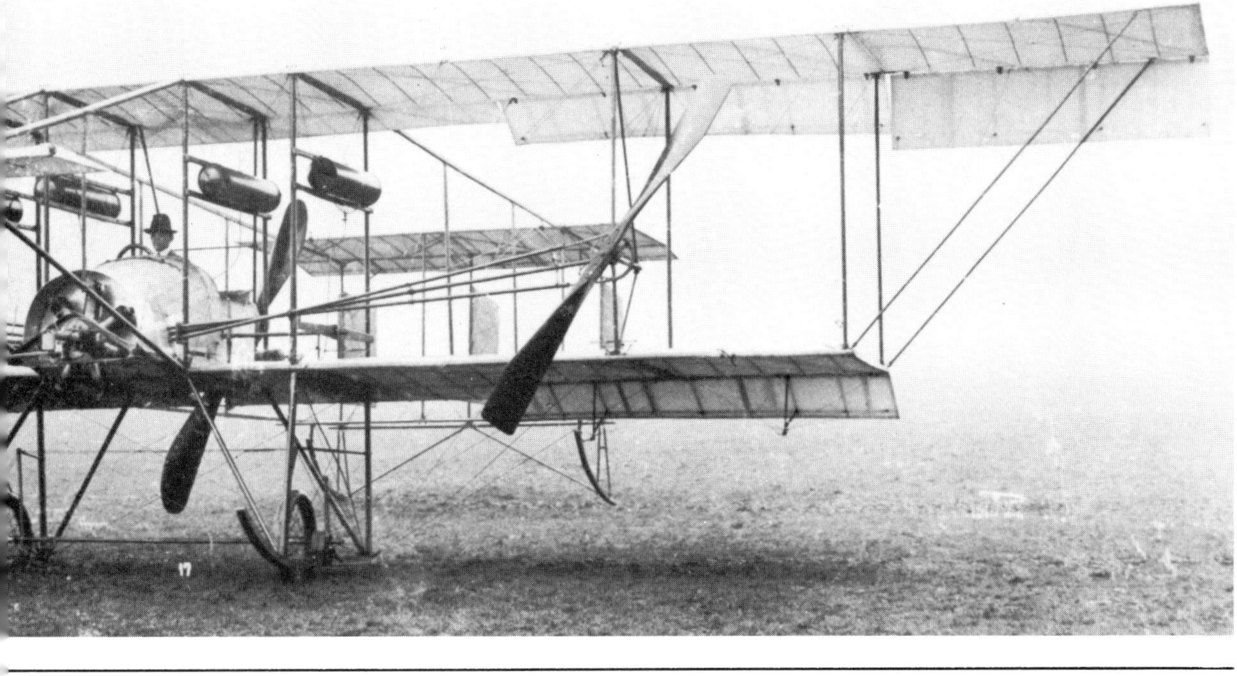

3 SHORT BIPLANE
S.78, 70hp Gnome

The Short Biplane officially numbered 3, although said to be T3 rebuilt, was a completely different single-engine pusher with the new Shorts number S.78. It appeared in June 1913, initially with an 80hp Gnome, and did much flying at Eastchurch, its Naval pilots including Samson, Marix, Osmond and Parker. By 6 August it had a 70hp Gnome. On several occasions in September 1913 Cdr. Samson flew it at night, and it was one of the Naval Wing aircraft that took part in the Army Manoeuvres that month. Shortly after the outbreak of war it went to Scapa Flow (where it flew a patrol on 25 August), spent a few weeks at Dunkerque, but returned, after repairs, to Eastchurch, where it was deleted on 26 April 1916.

5 SHORT BIPLANE
S.45, ex-T5, 70hp Gnome

The first photograph (right, top) depicts T5, marked as such, at Margate on 30 May 1912, shortly after being accepted by the Naval Wing. By 2 July it had the centre-float undercarriage seen in the photograph at far right and was flown by Lt. Spenser Grey RN, but reverted to wheels for the 1912 Army Manoeuvres. Damaged after a forced landing on 6 September, it was repaired, apparently with a modified wing structure. As a floatplane again it saw brief use at the temporary seaplane station at Carlingnose (right, below), where it capsized on 4 October 1912. (JMB/GSL; Philip M. Jarrett; Shorts)

4 SHORT TRIPLE-TRACTOR BIPLANE

S.47, ex-T4, 2×50hp Gnome

In the Short S.47 the two engines drove three tractor airscrews. The aeroplane first appeared at Eastchurch on 23 July 1912, and its designated Naval Wing pilot was Lt. C. J. L'Estrange Malone, who flew it frequently and participated in the 1912 Army Manoeuvres between 7 and 20 September. At Eastchurch it was used for experiments, including trials of a Rouzet wireless installation. It was damaged on 22 January 1913 and apparently was neither repaired nor reconstructed.

7 DEPERDUSSIN MONOPLANE
Ex-M1, 70hp Gnome

This French-built Deperdussin was flown from Paris to Eastchurch on 13 April 1912 by Maurice Prévost. Its first Naval pilot was Lt. A. M. Longmore. On 5 June, as M1, it arrived at Windermere to be fitted with a Gnosspelius float; this was officially accepted on 24 July 1912 but was not long retained. The monoplane was back at Eastchurch, on wheels, by 29 August, and took part in the Army Manoeuvres, 6–20 September. In 1913, as No. 7, it was frequently flown by Lt. Spenser Grey and Cdr. Samson, and was fitted with new wings in May 1914. After the outbreak of war it was briefly with the RNAS unit at Dunkerque, whence it returned to Dover in a transit case in October 1914. Although included in the December list of Naval aircraft, it seemed to find no recorded employment thereafter. (JMB/GSL; RAF Museum; RAF Museum)

8 SHORT MONOPLANE
S.42, ex-M2, 50hp Gnome

Completed on 24 February 1912, the Short Monoplane was put through its acceptance tests at Eastchurch next day by Cdr. C. R. Samson. He flew it a great deal that summer, as did Lt. W. Parke RN in September; Capt. R. Gordon RMLI also flew it. Initially marked 'M2', it later became No. 8 and saw some use at Eastchurch. Although cleaned, doped and varnished in September 1913 it deteriorated thereafter and was deleted before July 1914. (*Flight International*)

9 ETRICH MONOPLANE
65hp Austro-Daimler

The Naval Wing's only Etrich Monoplane left the maker's works in Vienna on 29 May 1912, arrived at Eastchurch about 15 June, and was test-flown on 18 June by the Austrian pilot Steugler with Lt. Spenser Grey RN as passenger. Most of its subsequent flying was done by Lt. R. Gregory RN. It had a general overhaul in late April/early May 1913, but it was not highly regarded and was dismantled during the week ending 11 October 1913. (JMB/GSL)

10 SHORT TRACTOR BIPLANE
S.41, ex-H1, 100hp Gnome (later 140hp Gnome and 135hp Salmson)

Short S.41 was first flown as a landplane by Cdr. C. R. Samson on 2 April 1912. By early May it had been fitted with a twin-float undercarriage, participating in the Review of the Fleet at Weymouth. Again as a landplane, it was flown by Samson during the Army Manoeuvres of September 1912; with its floats restored, it started flying from the temporary seaplane station at Carlingnose on 2 October (upper photograph). At Eastchurch a mounting for a Maxim machine gun was installed in mid-January 1913. During an overhaul in May 1913 the gap in No. 10's centre section was covered; in September new and folding wings of greater span and area were fitted, and the aircraft was flying in this form at Eastchurch in November (centre photograph). In early 1914 a 140hp Gnome was fitted; with it No. 10 was timed on 11 March to do over 70mph. A year later, still on the strength of the Flying School, Eastchurch, the aircraft was under repair in Shorts' works. By late May 1915 No. 10 was with No. 2 Wing at Eastchurch, where it apparently remained in mid-August despite the Wing's departure for the Aegean. By 2 October a Short landplane numbered 10 was in transit to that area, but this was a near-total reconstruction with an airframe like that of the Short Improved Type 74 seaplane and a 135hp Salmson engine. In the lower photograph it is seen at Imbros, allegedly in 1916; however, it was not included in the March 1916 list of Naval aircraft. (JMB/GSL; John H. Blake; W. Pollard)

The original SHORT S.41 Tractor Seaplane (100 h.p Gnome) at Carlingnose. Pilot - Commander Samson.   October 1912

11 HENRY FARMAN SEAPLANE
Ex-H4, 70hp (later 80hp) Gnome

This Farman was basically similar to the aircraft flown by Jules Fischer in the March 1912 Monaco competition for hydro-aeroplanes, which had been attended by Capt. Godfrey Paine RN and Lt. Arthur M. Longmore RN. It arrived at Eastchurch on 21 June 1912 and made its first flight a week later. Used as a trainer, it also flew at Carlingnose, where this photograph was taken, in October 1912; Lt. F. E. T. Hewlett RN is in the pilot's seat. A nacelle was fitted in January 1913, and by August 1914 No. 11 was at Grain with an 80hp Gnome, but the aeroplane was deleted on the 24th of that month. (JMB/GSL)

17 ROYAL AIRCRAFT FACTORY H.R.E.2
70hp (later 100hp) Renault

The H.R.E.2 was completed in mid-1913 as a landplane with a 70hp Renault, but by November a 100hp Renault had been fitted. Fleet Pond, where the aircraft was abortively tested on floats, did not afford an adequate take-off run; on 3 November it was flown to Calshot and floats were fitted at Hamble next day. It crashed on 24 November 1913 while being flown by Ronald Kemp. Flown again at Farnborough by Frank Goodden on 1 September 1914, the H.R.E.2 had by then been fitted with R.E.5 wings and ailerons, as seen at right. On 6 September it was handed over to FSL J. P. Wilson, who flew it to Calshot. Floats had been fitted by 15 September, but the aircraft was dogged by many maintenance problems. The photograph below was taken at Calshot. No. 17 flew a reconnaissance sortie on 1 February 1915, was fitted with bomb gear the next day, but crashed on 10 February and was not rebuilt. (Crown Copyright, RAE; JMB/GSL)

16 AVRO 501
100hp Gnome

The Naval Wing's only Avro 501 was first delivered in January 1913 as an amphibian in a clumsy centre-float configuration, but was not accepted. Modified to have a narrow-track wheel undercarriage, it was flown on its acceptance tests by F. P. Raynham at Eastchurch on 28 August 1913, and served there as a trainer. It flew to Dunkerque with No. 2 Squadron RNAS on 11 February 1915, carrying bombs intended for the Ostend–Bruges canal, but failed to reach the objective. It returned to Eastchurch and was deleted on 22 February 1916. (JMB/GSL)

18 DONNET-LÉVÊQUE FLYING BOAT
Ex-H7, 80hp Gnome

A contemporary note on this photograph states that this aircraft is the Donnet-Lévêque Flying Boat that was handed over at Eastchurch on 22 October 1912 by *Lt. de Vaisseau* Jean Conneau, but this identification remains unconfirmed. The aircraft, Britain's first military flying boat, was flown next day by Sub-Lt. F. E. T. Hewlett, and its brief career was spent at Eastchurch. It was not a success, and in the spring of 1913 it was wrecked in a gale when a tent fell on it. It was never repaired. (JMB/GSL)

19 SHORT TRACTOR SEAPLANE
S.54, 160hp Gnome

Short Seaplane S.54 was originally expected to have, and at first may have had, a 140hp Gnome engine, but by February 1914 it had a 160hp Gnome. It was then at the Isle of Grain, and on 15 May 1914 its passenger was Winston Churchill, First Lord of the Admiralty, his pilot being Lt. J. W. Seddon RN. This photograph was taken in August 1914 at Westgate, where the Short was damaged while taking off on 14 August. Repaired, it returned to Grain on 6 November, but was wrecked near Felixstowe next month. Its engine was salvaged on 15 December and it was deleted a week later. (RAF Museum)

20 SHORT TRACTOR SEAPLANE
S.57, ex-H8, 100hp Gnome

Recorded as being on order in November 1912, Short S.57 was one of two 100hp Gnome Short Seaplanes flown to the Isle of Grain by Gordon Bell on 22 April 1913. Used in early wireless experiments, it went to Great Yarmouth in July and did much flying there. Its activities included experiments with the GRW Wheel Attachment, a form of amphibious gear for seaplanes. This worked reasonably well, but not every landing was a success, as the second illustration shows. From Great Yarmouth No. 20 flew various patrols after war broke out, and on 18 November 1914 was fitted with a sight to drop 20lb bombs. On 15 December it went to the Handley Page works for overhaul, returning to Yarmouth on 12 February 1915. On 20 August 1915 it was despatched to Calshot by rail; its first known flight there occurred on 4 September. It was badly damaged on 31 January 1916 and was deleted on 14 February. (FAA Museum; JMB/GSL; RAF Museum)

26 ROYAL AIRCRAFT FACTORY H.R.E.3
120hp Austro-Daimler (later R.E.5 No.14, 120hp Austro-Daimler)

This number was first allotted for the H.R.E.3, itself a 'reconstruction' of Cdr. Oliver Schwann's Avro Type D seaplane. An unconfirmed note records that it crashed on 18 November 1913, but the photograph immediately right bears the date (also unconfirmed) of 3 December 1913. The H.R.E.3's replacement was the fourteenth R.E.5, flown to Hendon on 2 September 1914 by Geoffrey de Havilland. The other photograph is said to record its

departure from Hendon on 26 September, with Sqn. Cdr. A. M. Longmore as pilot; it arrived at Dunkerque next day. On it, Longmore and Flt. Lt. E. Osmond bombed Cambrai railway junction on 30 September. After repair at Supermarines in early 1915 it was with No. 4 Wing, Eastchurch, by mid-August. The aircraft was surveyed on 22 November for deletion, and it was transferred to the White City Depot next day. (Crown Copyright, RAE; JMB/GSL)

27 SOPWITH SCHOOL BIPLANE
Rebuilt as Sopwith D.1, 70hp Gnome

The aircraft originally supplied as No. 27 was a Sopwith School Biplane, apparently the second of two. Harry Hawker flew it from Brooklands to Eastchurch on 23–24 November 1912. It was expected to have a 50hp Gnome but apparently was delivered with a 70hp Gnome. Not over-robust, it returned to the Sopwith works in June 1913 and was reconstructed as a Sopwith D.1, the so-called Three-Seater; as such, it was flown by Harold Barnwell to Eastchurch on 6 November 1913, and did much instructional flying. In mid-March 1914 it was fitted with a gun mounting, but on 4 May FSL T. A. Rainey overturned in a forced landing near Shoreham, as seen here, and No. 27 was subsequently deleted. (JMB/GSL; Peter Liddle)

28 SHORT TYPE S.38 BIPLANE
S.55, ordered with 50hp Gnome (later fitted with 70hp Gnome)

Short S.55 was piloted by Lt. W. Parke RN on its acceptance trials on 4 November 1912, and was thereafter used at Eastchurch. It was fitted with bomb-dropping gear early in May 1913, an installation that was repeatedly modified and may have been superseded by the 'automatic bomb-dropping gear' fitted in mid-January 1914. No. 28 went to Great Yarmouth on 9 August, but on arrival was blown over by a gale; the wreckage was returned to Eastchurch. Repaired, it was at Eastbourne by March 1915, was unserviceable by 1 June, but after lengthy repairs returned on 24 November. The aeroplane was again in repair by 2 January 1916, and was still listed in March 1916, but it was deleted later that year. (J. R. Pennington, via KAHRS)

29 MAURICE FARMAN SEAPLANE
70hp Renault

This Farman Seaplane was in service by mid-1913, and was flown to Great Yarmouth on 18 July to participate in that year's Naval Manoeuvres. It was transferred to Grain on 29 June 1914, but later went to Calshot where, on 25 November, it was fitted with a bomb sight. It was unserviceable May–June 1915, but was serviceable again by 1 July. Transferred to Bembridge on 13 July, it was reported a total wreck on 25 July. (JMB/GSL)

34 SHORT TYPE S.38 BIPLANE
S.61, 80hp Gnome

Short S.61 was at Eastchurch before 10 May 1913. In mid-November bomb-dropping gear was installed, and by 6 December a 'sighting arrangement' had been added. On 15 December Lt. R. H. Clark Hall RN dropped many bombs from No. 34 (pilot Sub-Lt. R. E. C. Peirse), repeating this exercise on 17 December and on 13 and 21 January 1914. In mid-February the front of the nacelle was covered with transparent Cellon sheet, presumably to aid bomb-aiming, but the bombing gear was removed by 25 April 1914. No. 34 was at Grain by 5 September, where it was used in further armament experiments, and on 15 September dual control was fitted. It was deleted on 7 February 1915. (E. A. Harlin)

32 VICKERS F.B.5
100hp Gnome Monosoupape

The Admiralty first ordered a Vickers gun-carrying biplane on 19 November 1912, but the aircraft came to a premature end. No. 32 was basically an F.B.5, and was at Eastchurch (the locale for this photograph) in August 1914, armed with a Vickers belt-fed machine gun that had parallel-motion sights. On 12 March 1915 it was on the strength of No. 2 Squadron RNAS but was deleted shortly afterwards. (JMB/GSL)

38 SOPWITH BAT-BOAT
90hp Austro-Daimler

Following the 1913 Olympia Aero Show a Sopwith Bat-Boat was ordered by the Admiralty. The first aircraft delivered against the contract (CP32098/13) left the Sopwith works on 8 June 1913, was assembled by Hamble River, Luke & Co., and was handed over to the Naval Wing. In the photograph below it is seen at Netley on 16 August 1913. On 24 August it sank at Brighton and was extensively damaged while being salvaged. It never wore its number 38. The later aircraft, clearly numbered 38 (bottom), probably used the hull of the earlier one but had a revised tail unit. It was apparently in service by July 1914, its declared station being the Isle of Grain, but by 2 August it was at Felixstowe, where this photograph was taken. On 24 August it was sent to Scapa Flow and was lost there on 29 September 1914 when its bows stove in while taxiing. (Via John A. Bagley; the late H. F. Cowley)

39 BLÉRIOT XI-2
80hp Gnome (later 80hp Le Rhône)

The acceptance trials of the Naval Wing's first Blériot were flown on 26 February 1913 at Eastchurch by Gustav Hamel; his passenger was Eng. Lt. E. F. Briggs RN, who subsequently flew No. 39 a great deal. New wings were fitted by 11 October 1913, and an 80hp Le Rhône replaced the original Gnome early in March 1914. On 11 March Briggs set a new British altitude record (14,920ft). No. 39 went briefly to Belgium after the outbreak of war but, damaged at Antwerp, was returned to England and was deleted on 4 November 1914. (FAA Museum)

40 CAUDRON G.3
80hp Gnome

This Caudron, an Admiralty purchase, left Paris on 8 March 1913, piloted by Philippe Marty and bound for the W. H. Ewen Aviation Co. Ltd. at Hendon, who were the British agents for Caudron aircraft. It arrived at Hendon on 12 March, whence it was delivered to Eastchurch. It underwent an extensive overhaul from mid-July to mid-August, possibly in preparation for its participation in the Army Manoeuvres of September 1913, during which its pilot was Lt. R. L. G. Marix RN. The last official list in which it was included was that of July 1914. (RAF Museum)

41 AVRO TYPE E
50hp Gnome

This was an Avro Type E two-seater (later known as the Avro 500) that was delivered to Eastchurch early in March 1913. In mid-March it was proof-loaded before starting its training duties. During the week ending 24 May 1913 it was fitted with wireless aerials, and was extensively repaired and overhauled between July and September 1913. On 22 July 1914 Flt. Lt. H. E. Littleton crashed badly shortly after taking off from Shoreham, but No. 41 was repaired and delivered to Hendon on 18 September. It was there at least until 12 March 1915. (JMB/GSL)

42 SHORT BIPLANE
S.60, 80hp Gnome

Short S.60 was exhibited at the 1913 Olympia Aero Show as a seaplane and was bought by the Admiralty. On 12 July 1913 it arrived at the temporary Naval Wing station at Leven, where this photograph (right) was taken four days later. In subsequent flying it suffered various injuries to its float undercarriage, and on 20 January 1914, at St. Andrews (where, on another occasion, the photograph at far right, top, was taken), the floats were badly damaged and were replaced by a wheel undercarriage. As a landplane (far right, bottom) No. 42 languished for some weeks at Montrose, but by the end of February was flying at Dundee. Floats were again fitted for participation in naval manoeuvres in March–April 1914, after which the Short returned to Dundee. It went to Ostend as a landplane on 27 August 1914, but on 28 September engine failure on take-off compelled Cdr. Samson to fly it into a tree. Beyond repair, it was deleted on 14 November 1914. (JMB/GSL; St. Andrews University Library; JMB/GSL)

43 BRISTOL T.B.8
80hp Gnome

The second aircraft from the camera in this photograph, taken at Hilsea in July 1914 during the Royal Review of the Fleet, is No. 43, an early T.B.8 that was at Eastchurch by 11 October 1913. Two days later, flown by S. V. Sippé, it passed its reception tests and was taken into use by the RN Aviation School. Sub-Lt. T. A. Rainey crashed the aircraft near Leigh-on-Sea on 3 February 1914, but after repair by its makers it returned to Eastchurch. In August it went, via Felixstowe, to Killingholme, but later was at Grain, where on 14 November it was being packed for transport to Cedric Lee & Co. for repairs. It was back at Eastchurch by 20 June 1915 and remained in use well into 1916. (RAF Museum)

47 ROYAL AIRCRAFT FACTORY B.E.2a
70hp Renault

Numbered 46 and 47, two B.E.2as were delivered to Eastchurch in mid-April 1913. By 3 May No. 47 had already gone in for repairs and general overhaul, and No. 46 was likewise under extensive overhaul by 7 June. Both needed new wings, were returned to the RAF in mid-August 1913, and were rebuilt as B.E.2cs the following year. No. 47 was en route to Eastchurch on 24 August 1914, but proceeded to Dunkerque on 27 August. It was at Hendon on 20 December 1914, but on 21 May 1915 was transferred to Chingford, where this photograph was taken in September. Although reported wrecked on 28 January 1916, it was still included in the March 1916 list of Naval aircraft. (K. M. Molson)

48 BOREL MONOPLANE SEAPLANE
80hp Gnome

This was the Naval Wing's second Borel Monoplane Seaplane. Its delivery was confidently expected in the second half of March 1913, and it was aboard HMS *Hermes* early in July. On 23 July it was wrecked on board *Hermes* when she met heavy weather during the 1913 Naval Manoeuvres, but was subsequently repaired and used for training purposes. By October 1914 it had been fitted with a wheel undercarriage and was at the Isle of Grain, where it was deleted on 9 December 1914. (Colin P. Ross)

49 ROYAL AIRCRAFT FACTORY B.E.2a
70hp Renault

The first of two B.E.2as built by Hewlett & Blondeau and transferred to the Naval Wing from the Military Wing, No. 49 arrived at Eastchurch on 22 January 1914 and was tested on 26 and 27 January by Ronald Kemp. Its Naval Wing pilots included Lts. R. B. Davies and E. Osmond, the latter flying it to Portsmouth on 13 July 1914 for the Royal Review of the Fleet. After brief use at Immingham it went to Dunkerque on 27 August, was subsequently at Antwerp, and although reported deleted on 14 October it was still officially listed in December 1914. See also aircraft No. 167. (FAA Museum)

50 ROYAL AIRCRAFT FACTORY B.E.2a
70hp Renault

A favourite of Samson's, this Hewlett & Blondeau-built B.E.2a was at Eastchurch by 13 February 1914. It needed a new port lower wing before the end of that month, and had an additional fuel tank fitted in the front cockpit. No. 50 went to Dunkerque with the RNAS contingent on 27 August 1914, and in March 1915, as an aircraft of No. 3 Squadron RNAS, it was shipped to the Aegean. There it was flown at least until 10 December 1915, occasionally as a bomber. (FAA Museum)

51 AVRO 503
100hp Gnome

Three Avro 503s were delivered to the Naval Wing, initially as wireless-equipped seaplanes. The first, No. 51, arrived as components at Grain on 8 September 1913. Once assembled, it was tested by F. P. Raynham on 25 September and officially accepted. A year later it was at Eastchurch with a wheel undercarriage, moving to Hendon in December 1914 and being tested there by F. Warren Merriam on 2 January 1915. It went to Chingford for training duties on 25 May and was crashed on the bank of the local reservoir on 11 August by PFSL N. W. C. Blackburn, as seen in this photograph. It was deleted on 19 August 1915. (RAF Museum)

52 AVRO 503
100hp Gnome

The Naval Wing's second Avro 503 was delivered to Grain on 7 October 1913 and was put through its acceptance tests by Raynham. Like No. 51, it was at Eastchurch in September 1914 with a wheel undercarriage, and went to Hendon, where it was delivered in a dismantled condition on 29 October. It was flown by Merriam on 7 December. An official list dated 21 June 1915 attributes a 100hp SPA engine to No. 51 at that date. The Avro was transferred to Chingford (where this photograph was taken) on 18 September, and a list of 2 October gives it a 60hp Le Rhône. After use as a trainer it was surveyed for deletion on 19 January 1916 and dismantled. (JMB/GSL)

55 CAUDRON AMPHIBIAN
80hp Gnome

The first of two 80hp Caudron Amphibians was delivered to Grain on 12 June 1913 by Philippe Marty, who flew it from Le Crotoy. With No. 56, it was aboard HMS *Hermes* when she left Sheerness for Yarmouth on 7 July. On 28 July Caudron No. 55 was flown off a trackway on *Hermes* while she was making 10kt into wind. The aircraft crashed in the Medway on 15 October 1913 while being flown by Lt. A. B. Gaskell RN. Here No. 55, with engine removed, is seen on *Hermes*' hoist. (Colin P. Ross)

56 CAUDRON AMPHIBIAN
80hp Gnome

Delivered to Grain on 30 June 1913 by Sidney Pickles, No. 56 was flown by him next day on its acceptance tests with Lt. J. W. Seddon RN as passenger/observer. Taken to Yarmouth aboard *Hermes* on 7 July, No. 56 crashed on 14 July while being flown by Lt. F. W. Bowhill RN, and although the wreckage was salvaged the aircraft was beyond repair. This photograph was taken at Yarmouth shortly before the accident.

57 CAUDRON AMPHIBIAN
100hp Gnome Monosoupape

This Caudron Amphibian differed from Nos. 55 and 56 in having only a single vertical tail surface and a 100hp Monosoupape engine. Engine problems punctuated its delivery flight from Le Crotoy by Sidney Pickles, with his mother as passenger; eventually it was delivered to Grain on 6 August 1913 by W. H. Ewen, who is seen here with the aircraft. It was damaged on 25 August and was repaired. When Baumann was taking off on 15 October to put the Caudron through its acceptance tests it struck a buoy in the Medway and overturned. Although retrieved, it was not again repaired and was not accepted. (JMB/GSL)

58 SOPWITH HT SEAPLANE
100hp Anzani

The first of three seaplanes of this type, No. 58 passed acceptance tests at Calshot on 28 June 1913 and was taken over by Lt. Spenser Grey RN. On 3 March 1914, fitted with a new, lifting tailplane, it was tested by Howard Pixton. Bomb-dropping gear was fitted by 6 May, and on 25 June it was demonstrated with new floats designed at the National Physical Laboratory. Given a wheel undercarriage later that summer, No. 58 arrived at Hendon on 25 September 1914 and went to Dunkerque two days later. It returned to Eastchurch on 2 November, went to Yarmouth, crashed on 19 November, and was deleted on 9 January 1915. (FAA Museum)

59 SOPWITH HT SEAPLANE
100hp Anzani

The second Sopwith HT was delivered to Cromarty by lorry on 19 July 1913. It was first flown there on 23 July but sustained early damage. It was more extensively damaged on 3 September, and its major parts left Cromarty on 23 and 24 September for repair at the Sopwith works. By February 1914 it was at Grain; on 21 August Flt. Cdr. H. R. Busteed tested it as a landplane, and it was used in experiments with Holt parachute flares on 29 August. This photograph was taken at Eastchurch shortly before No. 59 left for France. It crashed on the way on 7 September and was deleted on 1 October 1914. (Peter Liddle)

60 SOPWITH HT SEAPLANE
100hp Anzani

This Sopwith HT was officially taken over at Yarmouth during the week ending 2 August 1913. The photograph records its return to Yarmouth from a flight by Lt. C. L. Courtney RN. It was last reported flying on 1 April 1914: after flights by Lt. Courtney and Lt. W. G. Sitwell RN a float was damaged during an attempted take-off by Lt. R. J. Bone RN. Overall damage must have been more extensive, however, for the aircraft was burnt in May 1914. (JMB/GSL)

62 SHORT TYPE S.38 BIPLANE
S.66, 50hp (later 70hp) Gnome

Flown at Eastchurch on 28 July 1913 with (as seen here) Shorts works number S.66 its only marking, and later numbered 62, this dual-control pusher was used at the RN Aviation School, Eastchurch. New wings were fitted in mid-September, and experimental floats were made for No. 62 in December but were probably transferred to No. 65. On 7 February 1914 a gale overturned No. 62; it went back to Shorts for repair, returning to Eastchurch in mid-May. Apart from a brief detachment to Immingham in August, it remained at Eastchurch until deleted on 22 February 1916. (FAA Museum)

65 SHORT TYPE S.38 BIPLANE
S.75, 80hp Gnome

This Short flew its acceptance tests on 16 September 1913, piloted by Sidney Pickles with Capt. I. T. Courtney RMLI as passenger/observer. The next day Courtney flew it to participate in the Army Manoeuvres, during which this photograph was taken. No. 65 was regarded as an experimental aircraft. Floats for it were under construction in mid-October 1913, and what may have been a further pair were in hand by 6 December. It was recorded as a 'hydroplane' in February–May 1914, and by 2 May work on its early installation of the GRW Wheel Attachment had begun. Later, No. 65 evidently reverted to landplane form, and it was used at Eastchurch as a trainer until 12 September 1915, when it collided with Caudron G.3 No. 3282. (Peter Liddle)

66 SHORT TYPE S.38 BIPLANE
S.77, 80hp Gnome

Short S.77 was flown at Eastchurch on 24 September 1913 by Gordon Bell with, significantly, Lt. R. H. Clark Hall RN, the Naval Wing's leading armament practitioner, as his passenger/observer. Two days later, as No. 66, it was flown by several Naval Wing officers. By 18 December it was recognized as a gun-carrier and was reported to be 'an S.38 type . . . but without front elevator, passenger in front, with a small Maxim'; here, with Winston Churchill (centre) and Cdr. Samson (right), No. 66 exhibits its Maxim. The aeroplane was used to test experimental gun and wireless installations, and when the war started it was armed with grenades and bombs. Its designated base remained Eastchurch; it was there in March 1915 but was no longer listed by the end of May. (Imperial War Museum)

67 MAURICE FARMAN S.7
70hp Renault

This Farman Longhorn was at Great Yarmouth when the 1913 Naval Manoeuvres began on 23 July, and flew several reconnaissance sorties. In February 1914 it was based at Felixstowe, and on 15 August was fitted with bomb racks. After repairs necessitated by a crash on 29 August it reappeared at Hendon on 15 November and remained there at least until 17 April 1915. It was at Chingford by 1 May; it was undergoing overhaul there on 16 February 1916; and it was still in commission in January 1917. (E. F. Cheesman)

69 MAURICE FARMAN S.7
70hp Renault

No. 69 was the first aeroplane to be delivered to the new naval air station at Great Yarmouth, and was flown there from Hendon by Lt. C. L. Courtney RN on 31 May 1913. The first photograph was taken shortly after its arrival and shows the Farman unmarked. Damaged in a forced landing in March 1914, it was sent to the Aircraft Manufacturing Co. at Hendon for repair, returning to Yarmouth on 10 August. By 11 March 1915 it was at the Naval Flying School at Eastchurch, but had moved to Eastbourne by 21 April. There it crashed on 17 May 1915 and was deleted. (RAF Museum; JMB/GSL)

70 MAURICE FARMAN S.7
70hp Renault

'A new Admiralty Maurice Farman' reported at Hendon on 26 July 1913 may have been the S.7 that became No. 70. There can be little doubt that the Farman flown on 6 September by Lt. Spenser Grey was No. 70, and it had reached Eastchurch by the end of that month. On 10 August 1914 it was at Felixstowe, on 15 August was fitted with bombs, and next day was sent out with bombs and a rifle. It returned to Eastchurch on 22 September and, despite several periods of repair, was still flying in May 1916. (RAF Museum)

73 MAURICE FARMAN SEAPLANE
70hp Renault

Two Maurice Farman Seaplanes were delivered to Grain on 16 August 1913 to become Nos. 72 and 73. The latter passed its acceptance trials on 22 August, flown by Lt. J. W. Seddon RN. On 24 September 1913, marked '73', it was used in 'experiments in shooting at aerial targets': these were wild duck, the bag two. On 9 September 1914 No. 73 was delivered engineless to Calshot. By 1 July 1915 it had been detached to Bembridge, returning to Calshot on 5 July. It remained serviceable until 31 December 1915 but was deleted on 1 January 1916. (JMB/GSL)

74 SHORT SEAPLANE
Admiralty Type 74, S.69, 100hp Gnome

This Short's earliest known flight (by Gordon Bell) was recorded on 19 January 1914 from Eastchurch, whence it went to Grain but may have returned to Eastchurch before final delivery to Grain on 27 January. Soon assigned to Dundee, it was being erected at Leven during the week ending 21 March 1914, in time to take part in the Naval Manoeuvres, after which it flew to Dundee on 21 April. It arrived at Calshot, for the Royal Review, on 13 July, and thence went to Grain on 28–29 July. On 23 August it left Sheerness aboard the SS *Indrani*, bound for Scapa Flow. It was recorded as 'ready' at Scapa on 30 August, but on 20 November was shipped to Grain and thence to the Handley Page works for repair. It returned to Grain on 29 December 1914 and was deleted on 30 March 1915. (M. H. Goodall)

75 SHORT SEAPLANE
Admiralty Type 74, S.70, 100hp Gnome

This was probably the Short tractor flown by Gordon Bell at Eastchurch on 31 January 1914 and to Grain on 2 February. By 23 March it was at Leven, and it went to Dundee on 21 April. It was at Calshot for the Royal Review and flew to Grain on 28–29 July. When war came it flew several patrols from Clacton and Westgate, and at least one of these took it across the Channel, for Nos. 75 and 76 were brought back to Sheerness from Ostend on 23 August aboard the SS *Empress*, apparently for repair. On 22 September 75 was on the move to Dundee again, by train; it was 'ready' there on 25 November and moved south to Granton the next day, but was dismantled on 7 December to go to Blackburns for overhaul. Sent back to Dundee late in January 1915, it was reported 'ready' on 22 February. It had been deleted before the end of May 1915. (JMB/GSL)

76 SHORT SEAPLANE
Admiralty Type 74, S.71, 100hp Gnome

In February 1914 the designated station for No. 76, as for Nos. 74, 75 and 77, was Grain. Its stay there was interrupted by reconstruction that spring, but it was flying again early in June, and went to Calshot for the Royal Review, flying on to Grain 28–29 July. On 2 August it was at Clacton; with No. 75 it was brought back from Ostend on 23 August, and on 21 September it began a rail journey to Dundee. It was dismantled with No. 75 at Granton on 7 December, was sent to Blackburns for overhaul, and returned to Dundee on 30 January 1915. It was wrecked on 22 February, and although listed as unserviceable at Dundee on 12 March 1915 it may not have been repaired. (JMB/GSL)

77 SHORT SEAPLANE
Admiralty Type 74, S.72, 100hp Gnome

From its initial station at Grain, No. 77 went to Leven for the 1914 Naval Manoeuvres, and was erected there during the week ending 21 March 1914. Maj. R. Gordon RMLI flew it to Dundee on 20 April. On 13 July it arrived at Calshot for the Royal Review, and flew to Grain on 28 July. It was at Clacton on 2 August, went to Ostend on 14 August, and was back at Grain by 22 August. Next day it left Sheerness aboard the SS *Indrani*, and was reported 'ready' at Scapa Flow on 30 August. It failed to return from a patrol on 29 September; its crew had been Flt. Lts. H. D. Vernon and B. D. Ash. (JMB/GSL)

78 SHORT TRACTOR SEAPLANE
S.73, 160hp Gnome

Shorts Nos. 78 and 79 were basically similar to their predecessors, Nos. 74–77, but had the 160hp two-row Gnome engine with exhaust funnel. No. 78 may have been the 160hp Short on which Lt. J. W. Seddon RN flew Winston Churchill from Tilbury Fort to Grain on 7 February 1914: the aircraft was listed at Grain that month. On 9 August it flew a patrol to Ostend. Preparation for shipment to Dundee was ordered on 12 September 1914, and the aircraft was still in commission there in December 1915.
(JMB/GSL)

79 SHORT TRACTOR SEAPLANE
S.74, 160hp Gnome

This was probably the 160hp Short Seaplane that Gordon Bell delivered to Grain on 11 March 1914. Although reported at Felixstowe in April, Grain was its recorded station from July to September. On 10 August engine trouble terminated its cross-channel patrol at Dunkerque. It left Grain for Dundee on 21 September, but was lost at sea on 1 January 1915. Its crew, Lts. H. A. Busk and L. H. Strain, were rescued. This photograph, probably taken at Dundee, shows No. 79 marked with a full white ensign.
(RAF Museum)

80 SHORT PUSHER SEAPLANE
S.79, 100hp Gnome Monosoupape

This side-by-side, dual-control, two-seat pusher was listed at Grain in February 1914 but did nothing of note and was dismantled for a time. It had been re-erected for instructional use by 4 January 1915 and flew occasionally and with difficulty. It flew a patrol on 12 February. On 30 May it was transferred to Calshot, where it was 'completely wrecked' on 24 August 1915. In the past this aircraft has been incorrectly identified as Frank McClean's Nile seaplane S.80, which became No. 905 in the Royal Naval Air Service. (FAA Museum)

81 SHORT FOLDER SEAPLANE
S.64, 160hp Gnome

The first Short Folder for the Naval Wing passed its acceptance tests on 17 July 1913 and was put on board HMS *Hermes* for the 1913 Naval Manoeuvres. It was damaged aboard *Hermes* on 22 July when a gale blew down its canvas shelter, and it went to Grain for repair on 29 July. While being flown by Lt. F. W. Bowhill RN off Cromarty on 4 September 1913, its rudder jammed at 1,000ft and the aircraft dived into the sea and was badly damaged. After repair it was used at Grain until wrecked in May 1914. (Colin P. Ross)

82 SHORT FOLDER SEAPLANE
S.65, 160hp Gnome

Tested by Gordon Bell on 2 October 1913, the Naval Wing's second Short Folder was at Grain the next month. On 21 January 1914 it was sent by rail to Plymouth but was back at Grain by 7 February. On 27 June it was delivered to Calshot by road, was tested by Gordon Bell on 6 July and took part in the Royal Review on 18 July. It left Calshot on 22 July for Grain, whence it flew a few patrols in August; it was apparently with HMS *Riviera* in September but subsequently went to HMS *Hermes* and was lost with that ship when she was sunk on 30 October 1914. (Shorts)

83 BOREL MONOPLANE SEAPLANE
80hp Gnome

Taken on strength at Calshot during the week ending 26 July 1913, No. 83 was flown in August and September by Sub-Lt. J. L. Travers. New wings were fitted during the week ending 6 December 1913. It was listed on Calshot's strength until August 1914, but September's list recorded it as a landplane at Eastchurch. It was deleted on 9 December 1914. (P. H. T. Green)

85 BOREL MONOPLANE SEAPLANE
80hp Gnome

Here No. 85 is seen at Cromarty on 3 October 1913, with Lt. A. M. Longmore about to fly with Admiral Sir Stanley Colville as his passenger. This Borel had arrived at Cromarty on 23 July 1913 and passed acceptance tests on 31 July. It went to Fort George on 4

November 1913 following the closure of Cromarty; it was listed at Fort George in February, July and August 1914, but in September was reported at Eastchurch as a landplane. It was deleted on 9 December 1914. (National Maritime Museum)

86 BOREL MONOPLANE SEAPLANE
80hp Gnome

This Borel arrived at Leven on 24 July 1913 and was tested on 8 August by Georges Chemet with Maj. R. Gordon RMLI as passenger/ observer. It flew during the Naval Manoeuvres of September 1913, and was subsequently stationed at Port Laing. No. 86 was flown to Dundee on 9 February 1914 and was detached to Leven on 25 March, returning to Dundee on 16 April. It was listed as being on Dundee's strength in July–August, but was at Eastchurch as a landplane in September. The aircraft was deleted on 9 December 1914. (JMB/GSL)

88 BOREL MONOPLANE SEAPLANE
80hp Gnome

Two Borels were delivered to Grain on 25 August 1913, the one that became No. 88 being flown on a 1hr acceptance test by P. H. Daucourt on 27 August. It may have been allotted to Felixstowe, the locale for this photograph, whence Capt. C. E. Risk RMLI and Lt. C. E. H. Rathborne RMLI took off on 22 October 1913 to fly to the Admiralty yacht *Enchantress* to meet Winston Churchill but No. 88 crashed shortly afterwards. No. 88 was not reconstructed. (JMB/GSL)

95 MAURICE FARMAN SEAPLANE
110hp Salmson

This was the aircraft flown by Louis Gaubert at the Monaco seaplane contest from 4 to 14 April 1913; in the photograph on the right it is seen flying at Monaco. It was bought by the Admiralty and was tested and officially accepted at Calshot on 23 June 1913. A crash that autumn necessitated repairs by the Aircraft Manufacturing Co., after which No. 95 had new wings of revised planform and enlarged rudders, as seen below. On 23 February 1914 Lt. Longmore flew it with Winston Churchill as passenger. It was flying at Calshot until 22 July, when it flew to Grain, apparently en route to its new assigned station at Felixstowe, and it remained there until deleted on 24 November 1914. It was still being dismantled for spares as late as 26 January 1915. (JMB/GSL; JMB/GSL)

96 HENRY FARMAN SEAPLANE
160hp Gnome

The Henry Farman flown by Jules Fischer at the 1913 Monaco contest, at which this photograph was taken, was bought by the Admiralty but crashed while still at Monaco, and its delivery was consequently delayed. Acceptance tests were flown by Fischer at Calshot on 28 August 1913 with Lt. A. W. Bigsworth RN and a mechanic as passengers. An official list dated February 1914 gives its station as Calshot, but it was probably no longer in use there by that time. It was deleted before July 1914. (JMB/GSL)

97 HENRY FARMAN SEAPLANE
80hp Gnome

Probably the first Naval Wing
Henry Farman with the so-called
Deauville sprung undercarriage,
No. 97 was delivered to Yarmouth
by Fischer during the week ending
24 January 1914. It remained there
at least until 10 August, but was at
Scapa Flow by 30 August. Shipped
to Grain on 20 November, it was
briefly back at Yarmouth by 12
March 1915 before going for
overhaul by the Aircraft
Manufacturing Co.; it returned to
Yarmouth on 3 April. It moved to
Calshot by rail during 9–16
November 1915 and was still there
in mid-February 1916. The second
photograph was taken at Calshot in
1916, at which time the aircraft
had its number painted on the
nacelle side. It appears that this
Farman was deleted before March
1916. (JMB/GSL; RAF Museum)

98 HENRY FARMAN SEAPLANE
80hp Gnome

Tested at Yarmouth on 11 February
1914 by Henry Farman himself and
by Fischer, No. 98 remained there
throughout its brief existence. It
was officially listed as being on
Yarmouth's strength up to and
including August 1914 but, having
been recorded as unserviceable on
3 August, it was deleted three
weeks later on 24 August.
(JMB/GSL)

103 SOPWITH D.1
80hp Gnome

On the Naval Wing's strength by 1 September 1913, No. 103 flew that day, piloted by Lt. Spenser Grey. Thereafter he flew the Sopwith from Portsmouth, Eastchurch and Calshot, which last was the aeroplane's allotted station from February to August 1914, though for much of that period it was under overhaul in the Sopwith works. Returned to Eastchurch on 17 June 1914 by Howard Pixton, it saw brief service in France in September. On 11 March 1915 it was unserviceable at the Naval Flying School, Eastchurch, but it visited Grain on 20 April; on 31 May, still on NFS strength, it was under repair at Grain. Although still listed in September it had apparently been deleted before 1 October 1915. (Philip Jarrett)

104 SOPWITH D.1
80hp Gnome

On 8 September 1913 No. 104, piloted by Harry Hawker, passed its acceptance tests at Eastchurch. The observer on the flight was Lt. R. B. Davies RN, who later flew the aircraft on a number of occasions, for example during the Army Manoeuvres of 1913. It is here seen at Hilsea on 28 July 1914 at the time of the Royal Review of the Fleet; four weeks later it was flying patrols at Scapa Flow, but it returned to Eastchurch on 5 September. It crashed there on 11 January 1915 and was subsequently deleted. (JMB/GSL)

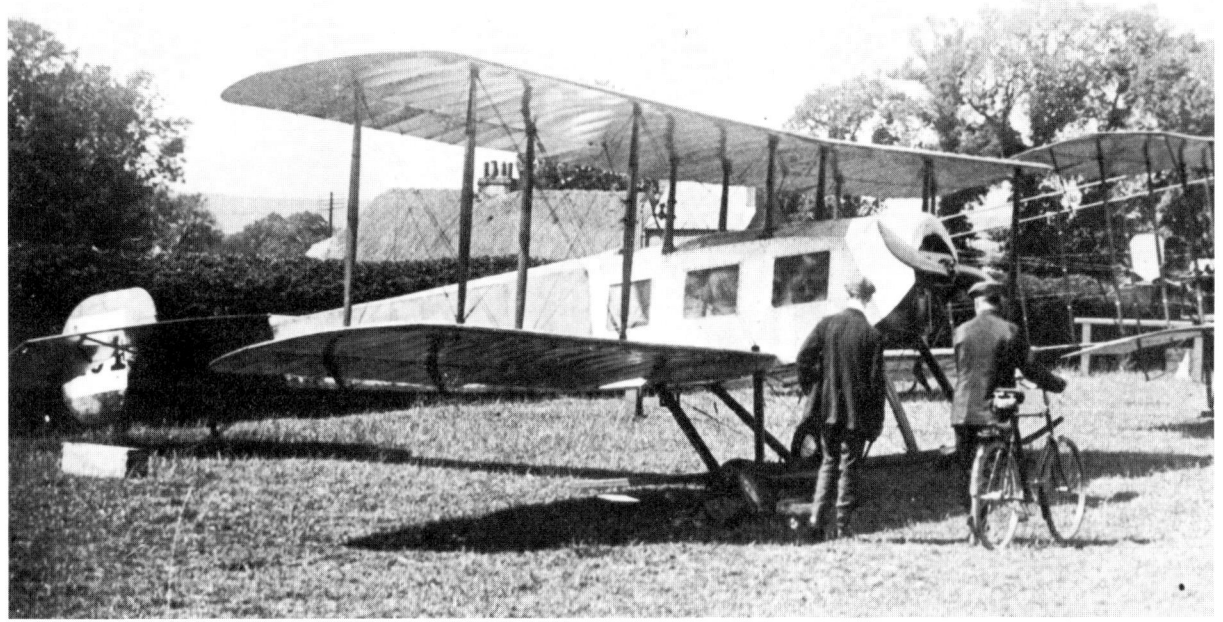

105 HAMBLE RIVER, LUKE & CO. H.L.1
150hp NAG

Already on Admiralty order in February 1914 with the 160hp Gnome as its intended engine, the H.L.1 was exhibited with a 150hp NAG at Olympia in March 1914; it is seen here partly assembled. Much out of balance when it was launched in May, its tail partly sank and it was badly damaged. Following repair, and with pontoon-type floats fitted, its flight trials were attempted, without success, by E. C. Gordon England on 11, 16 and 17 August 1914 and subsequently. It was never accepted, and was sold at auction for £30 in June 1915; the wings were bought by Pemberton Billing Ltd. for five shillings. (JMB/GSL)

113 MAURICE FARMAN SEAPLANE
100hp Renault

This Farman arrived at Felixstowe on 18 December 1913 and was at Calshot from 11 to 22 July 1914 for that summer's Royal Review of the Fleet. By 1 November 1914 it was at Dunkerque, whence it was sent back to the Aircraft Manufacturing Co. for repairs on 3 December. It was being re-assembled at Grain on 26 January 1915, and returned to Dunkerque on 5 February. On 2 July it arrived at Calshot, where it was undergoing extensive repairs in November. Although being erected in January–February 1916 it did not appear in the March 1916 list of Naval aircraft. Here it is seen with its upper-wing extensions removed. (RAF Museum)

114 MAURICE FARMAN SEAPLANE
100hp Renault

Delivered to Felixstowe shortly after No. 113, this Maurice Farman should have attended the Royal Review of the Fleet in July 1914 but was prevented from doing so by a lack of engine spares. It went to Dunkerque on 5 November 1914, was sent to the Aircraft Manufacturing Co. for overhaul on 3 December, and returned to Dunkerque on 16 February 1915. It was brought down and lost on 31 May 1915. (K. M. Molson)

115 MAURICE FARMAN SEAPLANE
100hp Renault

This Farman was apparently at Felixstowe in January 1914. It arrived at Calshot on 10 July to participate in the Royal Review, but on 22 July, while en route back to Felixstowe from Calshot (via Grain), it developed engine trouble off West Worthing and was wrecked on alighting. Its crew, Flt. Cdr. C. E. H. Rathborne RMLI and Telegraphist Stirling, were rescued, but the aircraft was lost and was deleted on 18 August 1914. (JMB/GSL)

117 MAURICE FARMAN SEAPLANE
120hp Renault

No. 117 was an earlier delivery than Nos. 113–115. Its assembling at Cromarty was completed on 12 July 1913, and it was tested on 14 July by Lts. A. M. Longmore and D. A. Oliver. Here, in September 1913, it is seen (at right) with Borel No. 85 (centre) and Caudron Amphibian No. 55 from HMS *Hermes* (left). On 2 October 1913 Longmore flew it with Winston Churchill as passenger, and on 7 October it was completely wrecked, leaving 'nothing but the tailplane worth repairing'. No. 117 was deleted before February 1914. (B. Hansley)

118 SOPWITH BAT-BOAT
90hp Austro-Daimler

The Bat-Boat that, with a 100hp Green engine, had won the Mortimer Singer prize on 8 July 1913 was acquired as No. 118. Accepted at Calshot on 27 February 1914, it was fitted with twin fins by 11 May, and on 25 June Lt. A. W. Bigsworth RN made a successful night flight, for which a headlight (seen in this photograph, taken at Calshot) was fitted. No. 118 was in the Royal Review, after which, ordered to Grain, it left Calshot on 28 July but had to be towed back after engine failure at Hayling. Apparently it remained at Calshot and was fitted with bomb-dropping gear in November 1914, but it was dismantled from 2 March 1915. (JMB/GSL)

119 SHORT FOLDER SEAPLANE
S.82, 160hp Gnome

Four three-bay Folders, Nos. 119–122, were on order in February 1914 for the Forth area. No. 119 was at Grain late in May; it arrived at Calshot on 9 July for the Royal Review of the Fleet, returning to Grain on 24 July. After overhaul by Shorts it was again at Grain in September. It was on HMS *Engadine* from 20 November, took part (flown by Flt. Cdr. R. P. Ross) in the Cuxhaven raid of 25 December 1914, and went briefly to Felixstowe on 4 January 1915 and thence to Grain three weeks later. Allotted for Special Service, it went to Shorts on 14 March for preparation for shipment to Mafia Island for the *Königsberg* operation in April. No. 119 sank and was lost after it was brought down on 5 May 1915. (FAA Museum)

120 SHORT FOLDER SEAPLANE
S.83, 160hp Gnome

No. 120 was at Grain in mid-June 1914, went to Calshot on 9 July for the Royal Review, and on 21 July flew at Calshot with a dummy torpedo lashed to its floats. It returned to Grain on 24 July, went to Westgate on 2 August, joined HMS *Engadine* on 26 August, was back at Grain on 29 October and returned to *Engadine* on 20 November. Flown by Flt. Lt. A. J. Miley, it was one of the aircraft used on the Cuxhaven raid on 25 December 1914. Shortage of fuel forced it down, to be taken in tow by submarine *E11*, but it had to be abandoned and destroyed. (JMB/GSL)

121 SHORT FOLDER SEAPLANE
S.84, 160hp Gnome

Early in July 1914 this Folder was at Grain, and on 11 July it arrived at Calshot for the Royal Review. It was taken over by Calshot on 23 July, and was fitted with torpedo-dropping gear 23–25 July. With this Short, Lt. A. M. Longmore made the first successful torpedo drop on 28 July, and on 3 August he flew the seaplane to Grain. No. 121 went to HMS *Engadine* on 26 August, returned to Grain on 29 October and was fitted with bomb-dropping gear on 11 February 1915. It was sent to Shorts on 14 March to be prepared for the *Königsberg* operation. The tropical climate affected performance adversely, and No. 121 was burnt at Mafia Island on 13 July 1915. (FAA Museum)

123, 124 SOPWITH PUSHER SEAPLANES
100hp Anzani

Essentially similar to the pusher seaplanes built for the Greek government, these two Sopwiths, on order in February 1914, were delivered to Grain late in May. By 10 August both were regarded as 'emergency only' aircraft, their controls considered unsatisfactory. On 14 August No. 123 went to Felixstowe, followed on 27 August by No. 124. Both were fitted with bomb-dropping gear, 20–22 November, and No. 123 was briefly used instructionally, flying a patrol on 14 January 1915. Both aircraft were dismantled and packed on 20 January and were subsequently deleted. It is uncertain which aircraft these photographs show, but the second might be of No. 124; it has an enlarged tailplane with balanced elevators. (FAA Museum; JMB/GSL)

122 SHORT FOLDER SEAPLANE
S.85, 160hp Gnome

Grain had No. 122 in July 1914, and on 26 August this Folder went to HMS *Engadine*. From 6 January 1915 it was used for instructional flying at Felixstowe, but was dismantled on 21 January for shipment to Grain. It was fitted with bomb-dropping gear on 11 February, and was sent to Shorts' works on 11 March to be prepared for the *Königsberg* operation. In April it went, via Durban, to Mafia Island, where it was burnt on 13 July 1915. (Peter Liddle)

126 SHORT GUN-CARRYING SEAPLANE
S.81, 160hp Gnome

Built to carry heavy guns, No. 126 was delivered to Calshot on 25 May 1914; Gordon Bell flew its acceptance trials on 2 June. It was at the Royal Review, and in mid-July carried a 1½pdr Vickers quick-firing gun, seen in this photograph; on 30 July it left Calshot for Grain, where it was subsequently flown with test installations of Lewis machine guns and Vickers quick-firers. By January 1915 it had only a single central rudder, in which form it flew to Yarmouth 26–29 January. In March it was fitted with a dynamo, a searchlight and landing lamps; in April it was used in tests of the 6pdr Davis gun; and on 5 May it went to Grain. It was deleted on 20 October 1915. (JMB/GSL)

127 SOPWITH BAT-BOAT
200hp Salmson

Under construction in September 1913, at which time it was intended to have a 200hp Anzani radial engine, No. 127 was the subject of an Admiralty order by February 1914 and may have been the Bat-Boat exhibited (with a 200hp Salmson) at Olympia from 16 March 1914. It was at Calshot by 15 May, where it passed the official acceptance tests on 20 May but damaged its hull on alighting and could not be accepted. It was sold to Greece and left Calshot on 7 July 1914. In this photograph it is seen at Eleusis. (P. F. G. Wright)

128 WIGHT 1914 NAVYPLANE
200hp Salmson

Two examples of the Wight 1914
Navyplane, to be numbered 128
and 129, were ordered by the
Admiralty in January 1914. The
former made its first flight, piloted
by E. C. Gordon England, on 7 April
and passed acceptance tests at
Calshot on 17 April. New flying
controls had been fitted by 24
April. No. 128 crashed off Calshot
on 4 June 1914, killing Lt. T. S.
Cresswell RMLI and Cdr. A. Rice RN.
(M. H. Goodall)

129 WIGHT 1914 NAVYPLANE
200hp Salmson

Exhibited at Olympia (as seen here) from 16 March 1914 prior to delivery, No. 129 first flew on 1 May. On 22 September, with extra tanks and bomb-dropping gear fitted, it arrived at Calshot and passed its acceptance tests; it was expected to go to Grain on 30 September. By 11 November it was at Fort George, where it was reported engineless on 20 December. It was wrecked on 30 January 1915 and deleted on 7 February. (JMB/GSL)

130 AVRO 510
150hp Sunbeam Crusader

The first of five production copies of the Avro entrant in the 1914 Circuit of Britain seaplane contest, No. 130 was delivered to Killingholme on 6 December 1914, its first trial flight taking place on 21 December. It failed repeatedly to take off and was not regarded as satisfactory. On 10 April 1915 it was transferred to Grain, where it made a few flights. A new undercarriage 'for experimental purposes' was awaited on 19 May. The photograph shows No. 130 at Grain with a revised undercarriage and (apparently) Short floats, both main and wing-tip. A refit was called for on 29 July and the wings were sent to Avros on 27 August. No. 130 was not listed in March 1916. (FAA Museum)

133 AVRO 510
150hp Sunbeam Crusader

On 25 March 1915 this Avro seaplane was being erected at Dundee, where its preliminary trials were flown on 31 March. Thereafter, with few exceptions, it refused to take off with a passenger aboard, but some solo flights were made. Its floats were reconstructed in June and tested on the 20th of that month. On 3 September No. 133 was declared to be 'of negligible value'. It was sent to the Supermarine works on 26 October 1915 but had ceased to be listed by March 1916. (RAF Museum)

134 AVRO 510
150hp Sunbeam Crusader

No. 134 arrived at Dundee on 4 April 1915 and attempted its acceptance tests on 12 April. It flew a few operational patrols, but only without an observer: its longest recorded patrol was of 1½hrs on 3 May 1915, by Flt. Lt. C. Draper solo. A new engine was installed on 6 June and its floats reconstructed in August, but no real improvement in performance resulted. On 19 October 1915 No. 134 was ordered to be returned to its makers. It was no longer listed in March 1916. (RAF Museum)

136 SHORT FOLDER SEAPLANE
S.87, 200hp Salmson

On order in February 1914, S.87 was delivered on 28 August 1914 as No. 135 but was renumbered 136 in mid-September. It went briefly to HMS *Riviera* on 3 October, arrived at Calshot on 14 October and returned to Shorts on 30 October. Taken aboard *Riviera* on 22 December, No. 136 participated in the Cuxhaven raid of 25 December (Flt. Cdr. C. F. Kilner, Lt. R. Erskine Childers). It went to

Felixstowe on 18 January 1915, but on 31 January was sent to Sheerness for HMS *Ark Royal*, on board which it went to the Dardanelles. A float strut was shot through on 27 April and the repaired undercarriage subsequently collapsed, as seen in this photograph. Still listed in March 1916, No. 136 was deleted on 9 June 1916. (Peter Liddle)

137 SOPWITH TRACTOR SEAPLANE
120hp Austro-Daimler

Delivered to Calshot on 21 August 1914, No. 137 passed its acceptance tests that day. It was wrecked on 3 September while being flown by Sydney Pickles with FSL Lord Carbery as passenger, and was sent to the Supermarine works for repair. It returned to Calshot on 23 April 1915, but was again damaged on 11 May. While awaiting a new engine it lay unserviceable from 21 May until 16 July; it flew on 19 August and occasionally (but ineffectively) thereafter. It was deleted on 1 January 1916. (Philip Jarrett)

138 SOPWITH TRACTOR SEAPLANE
200hp Salmson

This Sopwith was delivered to Calshot on 7 August 1914, passing its acceptance tests on 12 August. On 25 August it flew with a dummy torpedo. Its wing stagger was altered on 28 August, and during the following two days it made several successful torpedo drops, further torpedo flights being made on 12 and 13 September. No. 138 was damaged on 28 October during

an attempt to put it on board HMS *Hermes*. It was serviceable again at Calshot on 1 January 1915, underwent several engine changes from January to May that year, and was tested with camera sights on 25 June. On 1 July it was at Bembridge and on 1 August at Calshot, and it was deleted on 1 January 1916. (JMB/GSL)

139 HENRY FARMAN SEAPLANE
120hp Gnome

Here seen (at right) at Felixstowe with Maurice Farman No. 115, this Henry Farman seaplane was at Grain in mid-May 1914. Flown by Lt. F. E. T. Hewlett with Lt. Cdr. de C. W. P. Ireland as passenger, it visited Yarmouth on 3 June and was apparently transferred there before 11 July, when it arrived, as one of the Yarmouth Flight, at Calshot for the Royal Review. No. 139 left Calshot on 29 July. From Yarmouth on 9 August it flew a patrol 'with orders to destroy any enemy's seaplanes'. Later moved to Scapa, it crashed there on or shortly after arrival and was deleted on 24 August 1914. (Gordon Kinsey)

142 HENRY FARMAN SEAPLANE
120hp Gnome

Delivered to Yarmouth on 4 April 1914, No. 142 was used in tests with wireless on 22 May, flown by Jules Fischer in company with Telegraphist Hendry; while at Yarmouth its regular pilot was Lt. R. J. Bone RN. For the Royal Review it arrived at Calshot on 11 July, afterwards departing for Grain on 28 July. In August it was at Scapa Flow, and while on patrol 24 August engine failure compelled it to alight at sea. The swell caused it to break up after alighting; the wreckage was recovered, but No. 142 was deleted on 18 September 1914. (JMB/GSL)

143 HENRY FARMAN SEAPLANE
120hp Gnome

This Farman was delivered with No. 142 to Yarmouth on 4 April 1914. Bearing the additional marking 'C4', it participated in the Royal Review of the Fleet, arriving at Calshot on 11 July. It left, bound for Grain, on 28 July, but had to come down at Dover with engine trouble. In this photograph it is seen beached at Dover. It crashed on 11 August 1914 while operating from Yarmouth and was deleted on 24 August. (Eric B. Morgan)

146 MAURICE FARMAN BIPLANE
80hp de Dion-Bouton (later 70hp Renault)

The aircraft in the first photograph (top) was at Hendon on 18 October 1913, having been brought there by the Marquis Jules de Lareinty Tholozan. It was virtually an S.7 without forward elevator, its engine being an 80hp de Dion-Bouton. It was reported to be at Farnborough by early November, and may have been the aircraft delivered to Eastchurch on 9 December by Pierre Verrier to become No. 146. In the second photograph No. 146 is seen at Yarmouth early in March 1914, with Cdr. C. R. Samson in the cockpit. By the nose is Lt. R. J. Bone RN; to his right are Mr. Horace Short and Lt. C. L. Courtney RN. In mid-September 1914 No. 146 was flying at Hendon; after overhaul by the Aircraft Manufacturing Co. it was serviceable again on 1 December; and by 11 March 1915 it had a 70hp Renault engine. Transferred to Chingford on 11 August 1915, it was still in use there in September 1916. (JMB/GSL; JMB/GSL)

149 SOPWITH TWO-SEATER
100hp Gnome Monosoupape

A side-by-side two-seater, this Sopwith was flown to Hendon on 19 February 1914. The next day Winston Churchill flew as passenger, piloted by Lt. Spenser Grey RN; the photograph shows No. 149 with Spenser Grey at Hendon. Churchill again flew in the Sopwith on 25 and 28 February. It spun in and crashed at Eastchurch on 25 March 1914 and had to be sent to Sopwiths for repair, but this was completed by late August. It was at Antwerp with No. 2 Aeroplane Squadron by 19 September, with additional fuel tank and bomb-dropping gear. On 22 September No. 149 was flown by Lt. Cdr. Spenser Grey in an abortive attempt to bomb Cologne airship shed; it had to be abandoned at Antwerp on 12 October 1914.

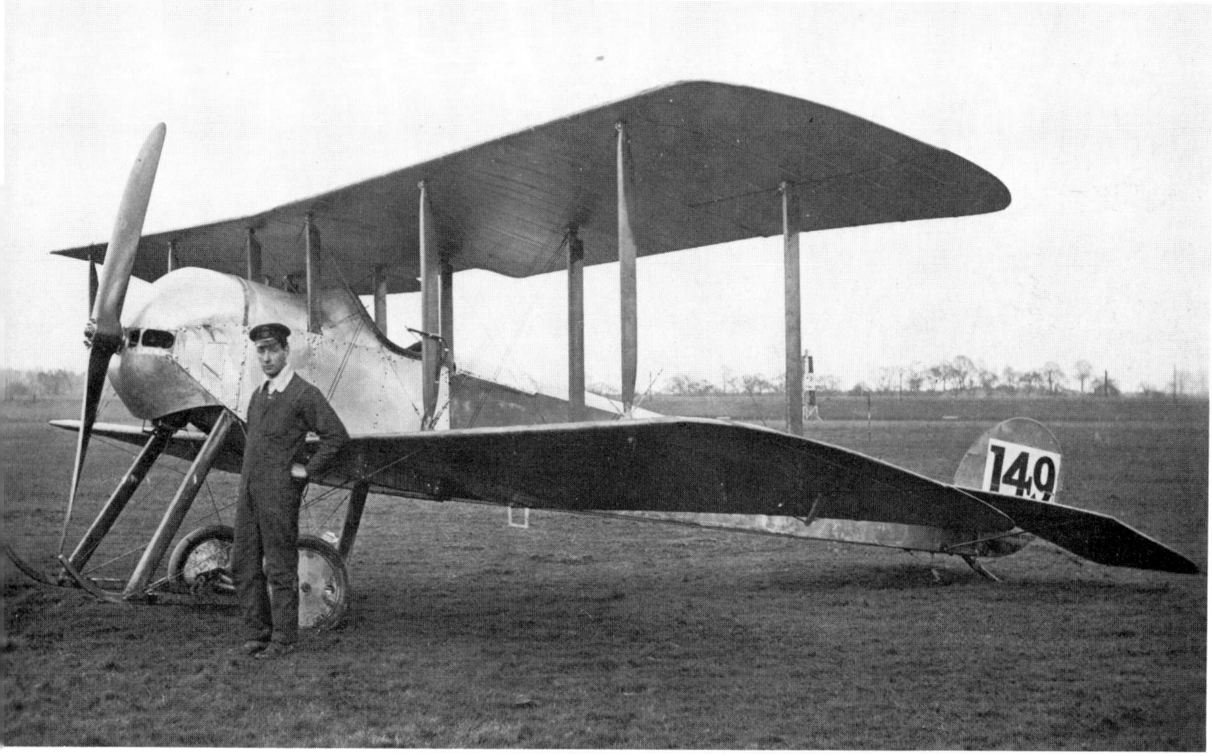

150 AVRO TYPE E/500
50hp Gnome

Delivered to Eastchurch by F. P. Raynham on 23 February 1914 and accepted on 7 May, this Avro Type E remained at that station throughout its brief career. Mostly used for instructional flying at the Naval Aviation School, it was one of the group of landplanes that were at Hilsea at the time of the Review of the Fleet in July 1914. This photograph was taken at that time and place. The aircraft was deleted on 1 October 1914. (JMB/GSL)

151 SOPWITH TRACTOR SEAPLANE
100hp Green

Built for the 1913 Circuit of Britain seaplane contest, in which it wore the racing number 1, this aircraft crashed on 27 August 1913 when nearing Dublin in the course of the competition flight. Rebuilt, it flew again as a landplane on 4 October, but crashed once more four days later. Again repaired, it was flying later in October and was subsequently acquired for the Naval Wing. It was tested at Calshot on 29 April 1914 and officially accepted on 12 May. The aircraft was at the Review of the Fleet in July, when this photograph was taken, but had earlier been reported to be 'entirely useless for observation work'. No. 151 left Calshot bound for Grain on 30 July, but engine trouble forced it down at Felpham. Having done little practical flying, it was deleted on 19 August 1914. (FAA Museum)

153 BRISTOL T.B.8
80hp Gnome

This T.B.8 was at Eastchurch by 11 April 1914, at which date a new undercarriage was being made for it. This was fitted in early May, and No. 153 was flying on 15 May. In July it was at Hilsea (the locale for this photograph) for the Review of the Fleet. By 22 August No. 153 was at Killingholme, but five days later it went to Belgium with the Eastchurch Squadron. It crashed on 13 September and was deleted on 2 October 1914. (RAF Museum)

154 D.F.W. MILITARY ARROW BIPLANE
100hp Mercedes

Brought to Brooklands in mid-November 1913 and purchased by the Admiralty, the D.F.W. was flown on 25 March 1914 by Lt. C. H. Collet RMA, who was its regular pilot thereafter. With a supplementary fuel tank installed, he flew (with Wick as his objective) from Portsmouth to

Humberside on 13 May. He flew the D.F.W. to Eastchurch on 3 June; it was at Killingholme by 23 August, was dismantled on 6 October, and left for Eastchurch two days later. It was deleted on 20 February 1915. (Grimsby Public Library, via P. H. T. Green)

161 SHORT TYPE C SEAPLANE
Later Admiralty Type 161/166, S.90, 200hp Salmson

Six Short folding seaplanes, originally designated Type C and numbered 161–166, were on order in August 1914. Here the first is seen at Short Brothers' works, wearing rudimentary camouflage. No. 161 was assigned to HMS *Ark Royal* by 11 March 1915 and was

taken on board on 19 April. It was still listed as in commission in March 1916. (Shorts)

162 SHORT TYPE C SEAPLANE
Later Admiralty Type 161/166, S.91, 200hp Salmson

No. 162 was delivered to Grain on 15 May 1915, but returned to Shorts on 20 May. By 20 June it was in transit to the Aegean, destined for *Ark Royal*, and by 1 October was on that ship's strength, subsequently operating from Aliki Bay, Imbros. Like No. 161, it was still in commission in March 1916. In this photograph it is seen taxiing off Salonika, where *Ark Royal* had been despatched in November 1915. (JMB/GSL)

163 SHORT TYPE C SEAPLANE
Later Admiralty Type 161/166, S.92, 200hp Salmson

No. 163 underwent its acceptance tests at Grain on 19 June 1915, and was subsequently sent to join *Ark Royal* in the Aegean. It is here (top) seen in those waters, colourfully marked and camouflaged, with Allied ships beyond. It was still in commission in March 1916, and, as the second photograph shows, was later fitted with a clumsy wheel undercarriage. (RAF Museum; JMB/GSL)

165 SHORT TYPE C SEAPLANE
Later Admiralty Type 161/166, S.94, 200hp Salmon

This Short left Grain for Rochester on 16 August 1915 and was subsequently shipped in SS *Joshua Nicholson* to the Aegean for *Ark Royal*: it was in transit on 1 October. It was photographed off Salonika, and also served with the RNAS at Mudros. It was still listed as being in commission in March 1916. (JMB/GSL)

166 SHORT TYPE C SEAPLANE
Later Admiralty Type 161/166, S.95, 200hp Salmson

Here seen on one of *Ark Royal*'s cranes, No. 166 had arrived at Grain from Shorts' works on 26 August 1915, and was shipped to the Aegean, with No. 165, in SS *Joshua Nicholson*. The form of the aircraft's markings suggests that this photograph was taken soon after No. 166's arrival on board *Ark Royal*. Like Nos. 161–165, No. 166 was still in commission in March 1916. (JMB/GSL)

167 SOPWITH S.S.1 TABLOID
80hp Gnome

Originally No. 394 (see page 125), this was one of three Tabloids bought by the Admiralty from the Military Wing in September 1914 for use in Flanders. Re-numbered 167, it was at Dunkerque by 16 September, and was flown by Lt. Cdr. Spenser Grey on 8 October 1914 in an attempt to bomb the airship sheds at Cologne. It had to be abandoned at Antwerp that same evening, and was deleted six days later. Here it is seen, engineless and in German hands, with the B.E.2a No. 49. (A. E. Ferko)

170 SOPWITH SPECIAL SEAPLANE
200hp Salmson

Britain's first aircraft specifically designed as a torpedo carrier was on order in February 1914, and arrived at Calshot on 1 July. Its first attempt to fly, on 6 July, failed; three days later, with an observer and with little fuel, it became airborne. It never flew with its intended weapon, and on 7 August was returned to Sopwith's Woolston workshop for modifications. It was back at Calshot by 22 August. Bomb-dropping gear had been fitted by 1 December, but No. 170 was abandoned. It was deleted on 11 April 1915, dismantling being in process from 25 April to 3 May. (FAA Museum, right; Mrs Helena Lloyd, via Charles Schaedel)

169 SOPWITH TABLOID PROTOTYPE
80hp Gnome

First acquired by the Military Wing as No. 604, the Tabloid prototype was bought by the Admiralty in September 1914. As No. 604 it was flown from Hendon to Eastchurch on 13 September by Harry Hawker with FSL Lord Carbery as passenger. Renumbered 169, it was at Dunkerque on 22 September and subsequently with No. 2 Aeroplane Squadron at Antwerp. It crashed on 25 September, had to be abandoned on 8 October, and was deleted on 14 October. (JMB/GSL)

172 WIGHT A.I IMPROVED NAVYPLANE
200hp Salmson

Wight pusher seaplanes Nos. 172 and 173 were delivered direct to *Ark Royal* at Blyth on 16 December 1914. Both flew on 17 February 1915 on arrival at Tenedos; No. 172 is seen here being hoisted out from the ship. This Wight made several successful reconnaissance/bombing flights over Turkish positions. It was deleted on 15 July but contributed components to maintain No. 175. (RAF Museum)

174 WIGHT A.I IMPROVED NAVYPLANE
200hp Salmson

Seen here in J. Samuel White's works with No. 175 beyond, No. 174 was tested at Calshot on 29 January 1915; the pilot was E. C. Gordon England and his passenger/observer Lt. Bramwell. This Wight had enlarged fins and additional drag bracing to the wings. It flew to Dover on 8 February, apparently intended for Dunkerque, but crashed and sank on arrival. (Michael H. Goodall)

176 WIGHT A.I. IMPROVED NAVYPLANE
200hp Salmson

Listed on 11 March 1915 as being in transit to *Ark Royal*, No. 176 reached the ship at Mudros on 5 April, having suffered damage while en route. Repaired, it flew on 16 April and saw quite extensive operational use. It was condemned as no longer serviceable on 14 July and deleted seven days later. (RAF Museum)

179 AVRO 504
80hp Gnome

Here seen at Grain in 1915 with its original 'comma' rudder replaced by a plain rudder with large fin, No. 179 should have flown in the Friedrichshafen raid of 21 November 1914 but could not take off. It joined No. 1 Squadron RNAS at Dunkerque in December, but by 17 June 1915 it was at Grain, being tested and fitted with bombing gear on 19 June and flying bombing trials on 4 and 18 August. Unserviceable from 11 September to 6 December, it was transferred to Eastbourne on 9 February 1916 and was still listed in March, but the aircraft had been deleted before the end of 1916. (Via C. H. Barnes)

183 SHORT SEAPLANE
Admiralty Improved Type 74, S.128, 100hp Gnome Monosoupape

Delivered to Grain on 24 November 1914, this Short underwent acceptance tests on 20 December and left for Felixstowe on 18 January 1915. It was used for some instructional flying in February and was damaged on 5 March. Although awaiting spares at Felixstowe on 1 June, it was reported serviceable at Gibraltar on 20 June and was still there on 1 October, but by March 1916 it was no longer listed.

184 SHORT SEAPLANE
Admiralty Type 184, S.106, 225hp Sunbeam Mohawk

On order, originally with the 200hp Salmson engine, in July 1914, No. 184 was delivered to Grain on 21 April 1915. It was flown to Felixstowe by Flt. Cdr. F. E. T. Hewlett on 30 April and joined HMS *Riviera* on 3 May, subsequently going to *Ben-my-Chree* on 21 May. Flying No. 184, Flt. Lt. G. B. Dacre made a successful torpedo strike on 17 August 1915. The seaplane was recorded as being en route to England on 1 October and was still listed in March 1916, but it was deleted before January 1917. (JMB/GSL)

185 SHORT SEAPLANE
Admiralty Type 184, S.107, 225hp Sunbeam Mohawk

No. 185 was delivered to HMS *Campania* by SS *Upcerne* on 20 June 1915; after assembly the seaplane was test-flown on 5 July and taken ashore. Back aboard *Campania* by 23 July, it was detached for mine-spotting duties at Banff from 18 to 24 August. It was damaged on 3 September and underwent repair ashore until 10 November 1915. It was no longer listed in March 1916. (FAA Museum)

187 WIGHT TWIN SEAPLANE
2×200hp Salmson

Specifically intended to carry the 18in Mk. IX torpedo, the first Wight Twin Seaplane was on order in July 1914. Completed in April 1916, it was delivered to Felixstowe on 15 July and was tested in August. It proved to be underpowered, was recommended for deletion on 1 September, and was deleted on 25 October 1916. (JMB/GSL)

200 SPENCER BIPLANE
50hp Gnome

Officially listed and usually identified, wrongly, as a Henry Farman (F.20 implied), this Farman-like pusher was the creation of Herbert Spencer. It was evidently acquired by the Admiralty in September 1914, for it was recorded at Hendon on 30 September and was flown by F. Warren Merriam on 3 October. Other pilots who flew it were FSLs. R. Whitehead and R. J. Hope-Vere.

It was officially listed at Hendon on 11 March 1915 and although still included in the September 1915 list of Naval Aircraft it had apparently been abandoned before mid-May 1915. (JMB/GSL)

Aircraft of the Military Wing

When King George V visited the
Royal Aircraft Factory,
Farnborough, on 19 May 1914, the
RFC lined up the Avro Type Es No.
291 and B.E.2as Nos. 336, 349, 239,
234, 368 and 329. (P. F. G. Wright)

201 ROYAL AIRCRAFT FACTORY B.E.1
Ex-B7 and B.E.1, 60hp Wolseley, 60hp Renault, 80hp Renault

Official documents indicate that the early number B7 was allotted to both B.E.1 and the Nieuport Type IV.G that became No. 254. B.E.1, designed by Geoffrey de Havilland and first flown by him on 4 December 1911, was handed over to Capt. C. J. Burke for the Air Battalion on 11 March 1912 and officially taken on charge by the Royal Flying Corps in May. It did much flying at Farnborough and Larkhill, and on 18 June 1912 it was re-engined with a 60hp Renault, the aircraft subsequently being used by No. 2 Squadron. By 3 April 1913 it was with No. 4 Squadron, was at Farnborough in the summer of 1914, was used in wireless experiments that autumn, and was fitted with B.E.2b fuselage decking and an 80hp Renault late in November. It was still in use at the Central Flying School in mid-June 1916. (The late H. F. Cowley)

202 BREGUET L1
Ex-B3, 60hp Renault, 85hp Salmson

Britain's first military Breguet biplane was delivered to Farnborough on 10 October 1911; it made its first flight in England two days later. Initially flown by Lt. G. B. Hynes, its later pilots included Capt. G. H. Raleigh, Lt. C. T. Carfrae, Capt. T. I. Webb-Bowen and Lt. A. G. Fox. It went to the British Breguet works for overhaul early in September 1912 but crashed on its return to Farnborough (pilot Albert Richet) on 7 March 1913. It then had an 85hp Salmson engine, was on the strength of No. 4 Squadron, and still bore its original number, B3. (JMB/GSL)

203 ROYAL AIRCRAFT FACTORY B.E.3
70hp Gnome

B.E.3 was the first rotary-powered B.E. It made its first flight (with Geoffrey de Havilland as pilot) on 3 May 1912, was taken over by the Military Wing on 13 May, and had been fitted with wireless by 24 August. Most of its flying was carried out at Farnborough, Larkhill and Netheravon, and it was a hard-working aircraft of No. 3 Squadron. Its flying career ended in the autumn of 1913, but it was still at the Royal Aircraft Factory, crated, in November 1914. (JMB/GSL)

204 ROYAL AIRCRAFT FACTORY B.E.4
50hp, 70hp and 80hp Gnome

Sister aircraft to B.E.3, this was first flown on 24 June 1912 (by Geoffrey de Havilland) with a 50hp Gnome engine. Flying with the Military Wing from 31 July, it was with No. 3 Squadron and flew during the Army Manoeuvres of September 1913. At Farnborough for repair and modifications from 23 November 1912 to 19 May 1913, it returned to No. 3 Squadron on 23 May. The aircraft crashed on 11 March 1914, killing Capt. C. R. W. Allen and Lt. J. E. G. Burroughs, and was struck off. (JMB/GSL)

205 ROYAL AIRCRAFT FACTORY B.E.2a
70hp Renault

First reported as flying as No. 205 at Larkhill on 12 October 1912, this B.E. was flown by various pilots of No. 3 Squadron, but was dogged by persistent engine trouble. On 16 November it was declared in need of a new engine but languished without one at Farnborough until 1 February 1913. Thereafter it flew with No. 3 Squadron, but early in May 1913 was flown to No. 2 Squadron at Montrose by Maj. C. J. Burke. There, on 27 May 1913, it crashed, killing Lt. Desmond Arthur. (JMB/GSL)

206 ROYAL AIRCRAFT FACTORY B.E.2a
60hp (later 70hp) Renault

Flying on 5 September 1912, this B.E.2a was taken on charge by No. 2 Squadron on 8 September. By 1 November it had an oleo undercarriage, and by 3 April 1913 was with No. 4 Squadron. On 18 December 1914 it joined No. 6 Squadron in France, returning to the 1st AP on 2 September 1915. It was still in use on training duties with No. 15 Squadron at Dover in November 1915. (JMB/GSL)

207 MAURICE FARMAN S.7
70hp Renault

Pierre Verrier flew this Longhorn from Hendon to Farnborough on 14 August 1912; after acceptance it went to No. 2 Squadron. When the squadron went to Montrose, Capt. G. W. P. Dawes flew No. 207 there, 13–26 February 1913. Probably rebuilt at Montrose, the aircraft went to Ireland for the 1913 Manoeuvres there; it was extensively damaged in a forced landing at Ballyhornan on 24 September and apparently was not repaired. (JMB/GSL)

209 HENRY FARMAN BIPLANE
70hp Gnome

Two precursors of the better-known Henry Farman 20 were taken on charge by the Military Wing on 9 July 1912 as Nos. 208 and 209. Briefly with No. 2 Squadron, both were transferred to CFS and renumbered, respectively, 412 and 420. The latter, written off from No. 2 Squadron to CFS on 7 December 1912, is here seen containing Maj. E. L. Gerrard RMLI. On 6 February 1913 the aeroplane was damaged while Capt. F. St. G. Tucker was landing in a strong wind and apparently did not fly again. (JMB/GSL)

210 BREGUET G3
100hp Gnome

First reported as under test by René Moineau at Farnborough on 17 July 1912, this Breguet was flown by Capt. C. A. H. Longcroft three days later but broke its undercarriage while landing. Taken on charge on 22 August, its use by No. 2 Squadron included participation in the Army Manoeuvres of September 1912; it was transferred to No. 4 Squadron on 21 December. Repaired after gale damage on 22 March 1913 and a subsequent mishap of 23 April, it was flying again in mid-May, remaining on No. 4 Squadron's strength at least until 19 December 1913. (Crown Copyright, RAE)

211 BREGUET G3
100hp Gnome

The RFC's second Breguet G3, also taken on charge on 22 August 1912, was first allotted to No. 2 Squadron but was transferred to No. 4 Squadron on 21 December that year. Its pilots included Capts. G. S. Shephard and B. R. W. Beor, and Maj. G. H. Raleigh, who flew it from Netheravon to Farnborough on 13 September 1913 for the Army Manoeuvres. During these it crashed on 25 September 1913, but the aircraft was still on No. 4 Squadron's strength on 19 December 1913. (JMB/GSL)

212 BREGUET L2
70hp Renault (later 85hp Salmson)

Originally delivered to Farnborough with a 70hp Renault by 27 September 1912, this aircraft was taken on charge on 3 October and allocated to No. 2 Squadron. On 2 November it was in the RAF for reconstruction and was transferred to No. 4 Squadron on 21 December, but it soon went to the Breguet works for repair. Back at the RAF on 17 April 1913, but with an 85hp Salmson engine (as seen here), it had done only 1½hrs' flying by 22 August, and although still listed by No. 4 Squadron on 19 December 1913 it never flew again. (JMB/GSL)

213 BREGUET L2
70hp Renault

No. 213 was taken on charge on 2 October 1912 after being tested at Farnborough by de Montalent. It did a fair amount of flying (various pilots) in November–December and was transferred to No. 4 Squadron on 21 December. Reported flying in February 1913,

it was badly damaged by a gale on 22 March; it may have been repaired (and possibly, like No. 212, re-engined with an 85hp Salmson), for 'an 80hp Breguet', unidentified but with a fabric-covered fuselage, crashed on 24 May 1913 while being flown by

Georges Collardeau, having 'just completed its acceptance trials' at Farnborough. No. 213 continued to be listed by No. 4 Squadron up to 10 October 1913 but may have been struck off before 24 October. (Crown Copyright, RAE)

214 MAURICE FARMAN S.7
70hp Renault

Taken on charge by No. 3 Squadron on 20 September 1912, this Longhorn was flying at Larkhill from December 1912 at least until mid-April 1913. Later re-allocated to No. 2 Squadron, it arrived at Montrose on 27 October 1913, and served there as a training aircraft for the squadron's pilots. Reconstructed at Farnborough in August 1915, it was with No. 1 Reserve Aeroplane Squadron on 23 August; two days later it was assigned to the 4th Wing, but this move was cancelled on 3 September 1915. (JMB/GSL)

215 MAURICE FARMAN S.7
70hp Renault

Apparently always a No. 2 Squadron aircraft, No. 215 was taken on charge on 17 October 1912 and flew frequently at Farnborough until the squadron moved to Montrose; flown by Lt. F. F. Waldron, it arrived there on 26 February 1913. It was reported, perhaps in error, that Capt. G. W. P. Dawes flew No. 215 to Ireland, 26 August–1 September, but it is certain that it was still in use at Montrose in April 1914. (JMB/GSL)

216 MAURICE FARMAN S.7
70hp Renault

An early Longhorn with the original, lower tailplane, this aircraft was taken on charge by No. 3 Squadron on 21 November 1912 and was flown from Farnborough to Larkhill two days later by Lt. G. T. Porter. It flew routinely with that squadron until 13 June 1913, when it was wrecked in a forced landing at Hengleton, near Brighton. (Crown Copyright, RAE)

217 ROYAL AIRCRAFT FACTORY B.E.2a
70hp Renault

Bristol-built, and taken on charge on 7 February 1913, No. 217 is here seen, with the early, unequal-span wings, near Doncaster during No. 2 Squadron's transit to Montrose. Its pilot was Capt. J. H. W. Becke, the date probably 23 February 1913 and the activity an engine change. Becke reached Montrose on 26 February. No. 217 later participated in the manoeuvres in Ireland, returning to Montrose on 26 September. Badly damaged in a take-off accident on 19 February 1914 (Lt. D. S. Lewis), it was struck off charge on 15 April 1914. (JMB/GSL)

218 ROYAL AIRCRAFT FACTORY B.E.2a
70hp Renault

Another of No. 2 Squadron's Bristol-built B.E.2as, No. 218 was taken on charge on 11 February 1913. As seen in the first of these two photographs, it had had the unequal-span wings when photographed at York on 21 February 1913 during the flight to Montrose. Its pilot then, and regularly thereafter, was Capt. C. A. H. Longcroft, who flew it to and in Ireland in September 1913. The outstanding achievement by Longcroft and No. 218 was the 430-mile long-distance flight Montrose–Portsmouth–Farnborough, accomplished in 7¼hrs on 22 November 1913; for this the B.E.2a was modified as seen in the photograph at far right, with a supplementary 54gal petrol tank in the faired-over front cockpit. The aircraft crashed on 2 May 1914 while on loan to No. 6 Squadron. (JMB/GSL; JMB/GSL)

219 BLÉRIOT XI
50hp Gnome

The Military Wing's first single-seat Blériot XI was presented to the War Office by the International Correspondence School on 28 January 1913. Its use was probably delayed by the monoplane ban then in force, and on 12 April 1913 it was in the Royal Aircraft Factory. Tested by Gustav Hamel on 24 April, it was at first intended for No. 2 Squadron, but it was with No. 3 at Netheravon by 24 June. It was flown during the Army Manoeuvres in September, flew at least until 23 October, and in August 1914 was sent to the CFS as a ground-instructional airframe.

220 ROYAL AIRCRAFT FACTORY B.E.2a
70hp Renault

Taken on charge on 13 March 1913 and intended for No. 2 Squadron, No. 220 was instead used in early wireless experiments at Farnborough. It went, probably only demonstrationally, to No. 3 Squadron on 26–27 May. Protracted repairs after damage on 2 December kept it grounded until July 1914, and on 31 July it was earmarked for the Aircraft Park that was to accompany the BEF to France. It went to No. 4 Squadron on 20 August but was wrecked six days later. (JMB/GSL)

221 BLÉRIOT XI-2
70hp Gnome

Blériot's tandem two-seat entry in the Military Trials (numbered 4 thereat) was taken on charge by the Military Wing after the Trials ended. It was in the RAF awaiting allotment on 28 March 1913, was tested by Gustav Hamel on 24 April, and was with No. 3 Squadron by 24 June. Its regular pilots were Capt. A. G. Fox and Lt. V. H. N. Wadham. It crashed on 31 October while being flown by Capt. Fox, and was struck off on 20 December 1913. (Crown Copyright, RAE)

224 MAURICE FARMAN S.7
70hp Renault

Taken on charge on 18 April 1913, No. 224 had been allocated to No. 2 Squadron by 8 May but probably did not join that unit. It was with No. 5 Squadron in August and was wrecked in a crash at Shorncliffe near Folkestone on 22 October 1913 while on detachment to Dover; its pilot, Capt. C. Mellor, was injured. (JMB/GSL)

225 ROYAL AIRCRAFT FACTORY B.E.2a
70hp Renault

An aircraft of No. 2 Squadron, No. 225 was taken on charge on 13 August 1913, and six days later Capt. C. A. H. Longcroft, with Lt. Col. F. H. Sykes as passenger, flew it from Farnborough to Montrose. It was based at Rathbane during the manoeuvres in Ireland in September, but it returned to Montrose late that month. Flown by Capt. F. F. Waldron, it left Montrose for the RFC Concentration Camp at Netheravon on 11 May 1914, but was extensively damaged in a forced landing in fog near York, as seen here, on 15 May and, although returned to Montrose, it was not repaired. (JMB/GSL)

226 ROYAL AIRCRAFT FACTORY B.E.2a
70hp Renault

Dated 2 August 1913, this photograph shows No. 226 at Farnborough shortly after delivery from Bristol. Although allotted to No. 2 Squadron, it was flown by Lt. W. Lawrence of No. 5 Squadron later that month in an attempt to set a new altitude record. Capt. J. H. W. Becke flew it to Montrose on 21–22 October, where it flew regularly until 28 March 1914, when Lt. L. Dawes set out for Farnborough. Once there, the aircraft was tested to destruction on 23 April. (Crown Copyright, RAE)

227 ROYAL AIRCRAFT FACTORY B.E.2a
70hp Renault

This B.E.2a was delivered in the late summer of 1913 but had only a short career. It was one of the Military Wing aircraft participating in the Army Manoeuvres of September 1913, in which it was flown by officers of No. 4 Squadron. On 22 September it crashed on landing at Lilbourne Camp with Lts. E. F. Chinnery and P. H. L. Playfair aboard. It seems that it was not repaired. (RAF Museum)

228 ROYAL AIRCRAFT FACTORY B.E.2a
70hp Renault

Delivered on 29 August 1913, this B.E.2a was with No. 2 Squadron at Montrose by 19 November. By 3 February 1914 it had been fitted with dual control, but this was apparently removed at the end of that month. Flown by Maj. C. J. Burke, it left Montrose for the Netheravon Concentration Camp on 11 May; its later journey to war began on 3 August, and Lt. H. D. Harvey-Kelly eventually reached Farnborough on 6 August. Maj. Burke flew it to France on 13 August, but it went to the Aircraft Park and was condemned on 11 September. (RAF Museum)

229 ROYAL AIRCRAFT FACTORY B.E.2a
70hp Renault

The Military Wing took this aeroplane on charge on 16 September 1913, and its early flying was done with No. 4 Squadron in October. By January 1914 it was at Montrose with No. 2 Squadron, and in 'C' Flight thereof on 31 July. It went to France with the Aircraft Park on 14 August, but was wrecked on 27 August 1914. (RAF Museum)

232 ROYAL AIRCRAFT FACTORY B.E.2a
70hp Renault

Built by Bristol and delivered to Farnborough on 5 September 1913, this B.E.2a was with No. 5 Squadron at Lilbourne during the Army Manoeuvres of that month, but by 22 October it was with No. 2 Squadron at Montrose. On 11 May 1914 Lt. E. R. L. Corballis left Montrose on No. 232 for Netheravon and the Concentration Camp, and on 13 August he flew it to France, where it was struck off charge on 15 November 1914. (JMB/GSL)

233 ROYAL AIRCRAFT FACTORY B.E.2a
70hp Renault

Delivered from Bristol to Farnborough on 20 September 1913 and taken on charge on 15 October, No. 233 was with No. 2 Squadron at Montrose before the end of that month. Capt. G. E. Todd flew it on 11 May 1914 to Netheravon for the Concentration Camp, and the aeroplane is seen here on Scarborough racecourse in July during the squadron's return journey to Montrose. Again flown by Todd, it went to France on 13 August. It was returned to the Aircraft Park on 5 November and struck off charge on 9 November 1914. (JMB/GSL)

235 ROYAL AIRCRAFT FACTORY B.E.2a
70hp Renault

This B.E.2a, built by Coventry
Ordnance Works, was at
Farnborough early in December
1913, and this photograph records
its crash there on 7 December
(pilot Norman Spratt). After repair
it was taken on charge on 6 March
1914 and was flown to No. 2
Squadron at Montrose, 10–27
March, by Lt. R. B. Martyn. He flew
it to Netheravon 11–29 May, but
No. 235 was condemned by the AID
on 9 June and struck off charge on
27 June. (Crown Copyright, RAE)

239 ROYAL AIRCRAFT FACTORY B.E.2a
70hp Renault

Vickers-built, No. 239 was
delivered to Farnborough on 29
October 1913, and was
photographed beside No. 206, with
R.E.5 No. 361 and the second
R.E.1, No. 608, beyond. Taken on
charge on 26 February 1914, it was

used by No. 6 Squadron. On 31 July
1914 it was earmarked for the
Aircraft Park but went to France
with No. 2 Squadron (Lt. M. W.
Noel) on 13 August. It was struck
off charge on 1 September 1914.
(JMB/GSL)

240 ROYAL AIRCRAFT FACTORY B.E.2a
70hp Renault

The tent hangars of the Military Wing's Concentration Camp at Netheravon provide the background for No. 240, a Bristol-built B.E.2a that had been taken on charge on 10 December 1913 and was equipped with a Rouzet wireless set in April 1914. On 31 July 1914 it was earmarked for No. 4 Squadron, and it went to France with that unit on 14 August. Two days later it was sent to the Aircraft Park, where it was struck off charge on 29 August 1914. (*Flight International*)

243 SOPWITH D.1
80hp Gnome

This Sopwith design first appeared early in February 1913 as a three-seater. Nine were ordered for the Military Wing, the first example flying at Brooklands early in November 1913. The aircraft numbered 243 was subjected to static loading tests at the RAF in January 1914 (this photograph is dated 31 January), and is here seen after failure of the port upper mainplane. (Crown Copyright, RAE)

251 BLÉRIOT XXI
Ex-B2, 70hp Gnome

While in the original ownership of Lt. R. A. Cammell RE, this Blériot was used in early trial installations of various flight instruments, compasses and a wireless aerial in June 1911. Acquired for the Air Battalion in August 1911 and numbered B2, it was damaged on 31 August. It flew and crashed on 6 December, was flying again by 10 January 1912, but went to Farnborough for overhaul late in February. Never satisfactory, it lay engineless at Larkhill from October 1912; a proposal to 'reconstruct' it as a B.E.3/4 was never implemented, although by 21 March 1913 it was at the RAF. It was struck off on 20 December 1913. (Crown Copyright, RAE)

The Blériot Monoplane.

252 DEPERDUSSIN MONOPLANE
Ex-B5, 60hp Anzani

This Deperdussin arrived at Larkhill on 11 January 1912, was flown the next day by Lt. John Porte RN, then of the Deperdussin company, and was taken on charge that month. It went to No. 3 Squadron, was used to test various means of signalling, including 'flaps' (flags?) and a siren. By October 1912 it was in the RAF, to be dismantled; it was still there in mid-April 1913 and was struck off on 26 November 1913. (JMB/GSL)

253 NIEUPORT TYPE IV.G
Ex-B4, 50hp Gnome

Purchased in September 1911 and taken on charge in November as B4, this Nieuport monoplane was regularly flown by Lt. B. H. Barrington-Kennett. On 14 February 1912 he flew it for 4hrs 51mins, covered a total distance of 249mls 840yds, and thereby won a Mortimer Singer prize of £500. By November 1912 the aircraft was on the strength of No. 3 Squadron and numbered 253. Its wings and fuselage needed new fabric, but the monoplane ban was in force: No. 253 never flew again, and it was struck off on 13 August 1913. (RAF Museum)

254 NIEUPORT TYPE IV.G
Ex-B7, 70hp Gnome

The Military Wing took this Nieuport monoplane (which originally shared the number B7 with B.E.1 – see No. 201) on charge on 19 June 1912, and it was allocated to No. 3 Squadron. It did very little flying since its fuselage was damaged in a landing accident on 14 August. By 26 October it was in the RAF at Farnborough, where it lay until struck off on 1 September 1913. The aircraft's total flying time was about 2½hrs. (RAF Museum)

255 NIEUPORT TYPE IV.G
100hp Gnome

No. 255 was taken on charge on 19 June 1912 for No. 3 Squadron, but it is doubtful whether, owing to the monoplane ban, it was ever flown by any RFC pilot. Apparently at Larkhill until January 1913, it was not wholly neglected however, for it was declared to need new flying wires in early November 1912. Although subsequently reported as serviceable, it went to the RAF late in January 1913 and was struck off on 5 August. (Crown Copyright, RAE)

256 BRISTOL-PRIER MONOPLANE
Ex-B6, 50hp Gnome

Delivered to Larkhill on 12 January 1912, this aircraft was tested on 28 and 29 January by its designer Pierre Prier, with Lt. G. J. E. Manisty as passenger. It was taken on charge on 17 February, crashed on 26 April, and was returned to Bristol for repair. Back at Larkhill on 20 June it crashed again; when rebuilt and handed over on 25 July it had a lengthened fuselage and a new tail unit. It flew with No. 3 Squadron until grounded by the monoplane ban, was at the RAF in mid-April 1913 and was struck off on 5 August. (JMB/GSL)

257 DEPERDUSSIN MONOPLANE
60hp Anzani

This monoplane was the personal property of Capt. Patrick Hamilton: when he reported to Farnborough on joining the RFC on 19 May 1912 he flew it there from Beaulieu. The War Office bought it from him in August, and it was assigned to No. 3 Squadron at Larkhill. Although serviceable, it ceased to fly when the monoplane ban was imposed, ended its days at Farnborough, and was struck off on 26 November 1913. (RAF Museum)

258 DEPERDUSSIN MONOPLANE
Ex-Military Trials No. 26, 100hp Gnome

Placed second in the Military Trials, this French-built Deperdussin was acquired by the Military Wing when the Trials ended. It was allotted to No. 3 Squadron and was one of the unit's aircraft that were to take part in the 1912 Army Manoeuvres. On 6

September it broke up over Graveley and its crew, Capt. Patrick Hamilton and Lt. Athole Wyness-Stuart, were killed. This was one of the fatal accidents that led to the monoplane ban of 14 September 1912. (JMB/GSL)

260 DEPERDUSSIN MONOPLANE
70hp Gnome

This monoplane was in the British Deperdussin works at Highgate on 15 October 1912; by 26 October it was on the strength of No. 3 Squadron but by 9 November was under order to go to the CFS. It was transferred there on 12

November and assumed the new identity No. 419, but the monoplane ban apparently led to its early demise. The number 260 was later re-allocated to a Blériot XI-2. (Crown Copyright, RAE)

261 BRISTOL-PRIER MONOPLANE
50hp Gnome

Acceptance tests of No. 261 were flown on 30 August 1912 by Howard Pixton, with Capt. C. R. W. Allen as passenger, and, taken on charge next day, the aircraft was allocated to No. 3 Squadron. Its participation in the 1912 manoeuvres was thwarted by a two-week wait for a new propeller to replace the original damaged in a forced landing at Farmoor on 10 September. Serviceable but under ban throughout the winter, it went to the Royal Aircraft Factory in mid-March 1913 and was struck off on 5 August. (Crown Copyright, RAE)

262 BRISTOL-COANDA MONOPLANE
Ex-Military Trials No. 15, 80hp Gnome

Flown with modest success in the Military Trials, both Bristol-Coanda monoplanes were purchased by the War Office. No. 262 was taken on charge on 17 September 1912 and allotted to No. 3 Squadron, but is believed to have flown only 15 minutes in RFC hands. By 26 October it was engineless, remaining so until sent to the RAF on 20 February 1913. It was struck off on 1 September 1913. (Crown Copyright, RAE)

263 BRISTOL-COANDA MONOPLANE
Ex-Military Trials No. 14, 80hp Gnome

After acquisition by the Military Wing this aircraft had the fin-and-rudder assembly seen in this photograph (taken during the Military Trials) replaced by a larger rudder like that of No. 262. It was assigned to No. 3 Squadron but crashed on 10 September 1912, killing Lts. C. A. Bettington and E. Hotchkiss. The second photograph illustrates the new rudder and, tragically, the totality of the destruction of the monoplane. (JMB/GSL; P. F. G. Wright)

265 FLANDERS F.4
70hp Renault

The first of the RFC's four Flanders F.4s underwent its acceptance tests at Farnborough on 8 November 1912 and probably became No. 422. The second was apparently handed over on 3 December, the third on or shortly after 18 December, and the last on 2 January 1913. It is uncertain which of them became No. 265, for it never went to a squadron and had evidently been struck off before 14 July 1913. (Crown Copyright, RAE)

266 MAURICE FARMAN S.7
70hp Renault

On 21 December 1912 this Longhorn was taken on charge and allocated to No. 2 Squadron. When the squadron went to Montrose in February 1913 No. 266 was flown by Lt. P. W. L. Herbert, and the aeroplane is here seen at Kelham on 20 February; it reached Montrose on 26 February. After crashing on 5 May 1913 it went to the RAF for repair, and may have been numbered 472 before going to the CFS. (JMB/GSL)

267 ROYAL AIRCRAFT FACTORY B.E.2a
70hp Renault

Built by the Royal Aircraft Factory, No. 267 was taken on charge by No. 3 Squadron on 18 March 1913 but was wrecked on 8 April and sent to the RAF for repair. On 23 October Lt. L. Dawes arrived at Montrose on it, and the aircraft flew with No. 2 Squadron until summer 1914, leaving Montrose for the Netheravon Concentration Camp on 19 May. By 11 August it was again in the RAF for repair, and on 14 October it went to Hounslow as a Home Defence aircraft but by 12 November it was with No. 1 Reserve Aeroplane Squadron on training duties. It was also used in that capacity by Nos. 9 and 10 Squadrons. (JMB/GSL)

272 ROYAL AIRCRAFT FACTORY B.E.2a
70hp Renault

RAF-built, No. 272 was taken on charge by No. 3 Squadron on 26 March 1913 and was flown by Maj. H. R. M. Brooke-Popham on 9 April. Reallocated to No. 2 Squadron, it was flown to Montrose by Capt. J. H. W. Becke 19–21 May and was flown to Ireland for the September manoeuvres, returning to Montrose on 1 October. It crashed on 4 June 1914 en route to Netheravon Concentration Camp; repaired, it was in 'C' Flight of No. 2 Squadron on 31 July 1914 but did not go to France. (JMB/GSL)

273 ROYAL AIRCRAFT FACTORY B.E.2a
70hp Renault

By 12 April 1913 this Bristol-built B.E.2a was at Farnborough, intended for No. 3 Squadron. Soon transferred to No. 2 Squadron, it was flown from Farnborough to Montrose on 21 May by Capt. C. A. H. Longcroft. In August Lt. F. F. Waldron made three attempts to set a new British altitude record flying this aircraft, and shortly afterwards it went to Ireland for the manoeuvres there; this photograph was taken at Castle Kennedy, near Stranraer, at the end of August, during the journey to Ireland. No. 273 was badly damaged while returning and was written off on 17 January 1914. (JMB/GSL)

274 HENRY FARMAN F.20
80hp Gnome

Although taken on charge by No. 3 Squadron on 31 March 1913, No. 274 spent a few weeks with the Flying Depot at Farnborough for experimental purposes. It was with its squadron by 23 May, and was usually flown by Lt. R. Cholmondeley until it crashed at Dorton on 27 August. It was flying again, with its pilot in the rear seat, by 12 May 1914, went to France with No. 3 Squadron on 13 August, and was wrecked on 19 September 1914. (JMB/GSL)

277 HENRY FARMAN F.20
80hp Gnome

This Farman was taken on charge by No. 3 Squadron on 10 April 1913. It was used in early experiments in photography and bombing in May, and its pilots in No. 3 Squadron included Lt. G. I. Carmichael, Maj. J. F. A. Higgins, Lt. N. S. Roupell, Lt. C. R. W. Allen and Lt. R. Cholmondeley. Its career apparently ended in a crash on 2 June 1913. (JMB/GSL)

278 MARTIN & HANDASYDE MONOPLANE
60hp Antoinette

Another of the victims of the monoplane ban was this handsome aircraft, purchased in August 1912, when its designated pilot was to be Lt. W. Lawrence. It was being tested at Larkhill by F. P. Raynham on 1 and 5 September, but may never have been flown by any Military Wing pilot. By March–April 1913 it was in the RAF, intended for No. 5 Squadron, but it was broken up at Farnborough and its remains were buried behind K4 Building there. (JMB/GSL)

280 DEPERDUSSIN MONOPLANE
100hp Gnome

In all, nine Deperdussin monoplanes were ordered from the British Deperdussin company during the financial year ending 31 March 1913; their total cost was £8,473. This one had the 100hp, two-row Gnome. Condemned to be grounded by the monoplane ban, it was in the RAF in March–April 1913, nominally for No. 5 Squadron, but was never delivered. (Crown Copyright, RAE)

281 FLANDERS F.4
70hp Renault

As in the case of No. 265 (q.v.), it cannot be determined with certainty which of the Flanders monoplanes became No. 281. An official directive of 1 July 1913 required all four to be transferred to the RAF for disposal; by 18 July

Nos. 265, 411 and 439 had been handed over for that purpose, but No. 281 was not then accounted for. Like No. 265, it saw no squadron service. (Crown Copyright, RAE)

282 NIEUPORT TYPE IV.G
70hp Gnome

In official records, No. 282 was listed as a two-seat Nieuport monoplane with a 70hp Gnome that was apparently on the strength of the RFC Flying Depot, Farnborough, in mid-April 1913. Among the aircraft purchased from Grahame-White in March 1913 was

such a Nieuport, which had been acquired by him in August 1911. After overhaul at Hendon it was not in fact delivered to Farnborough until 25 May 1913 (by Marc Bonnier), which perhaps impairs the possibility of its being No. 282. An alternative recipient of

that number could have been Robert Loraine's 70hp two-seat Nieuport, which arrived at Hendon on 2 January 1912, and was later purchased by the War Office for £400. Whatever No. 282's origins, it went to no squadron. (JMB/GSL)

283 GRAHAME-WHITE TYPE VII
35hp Anzani

Completed early in January 1913, the little Grahame-White Popular Biplane was one of the first aircraft to be designed as a light sporting type. The War Office was interested in it – probably before the official headlong rush to buy up aircraft to support Col. Seely's imaginative claims about the RFC's strength – and bought it in March 1913, ostensibly for No. 3 Squadron. No record of its actual use in the Military Wing has yet been found. (JMB/GSL)

284 HENRY FARMAN F.20
80hp Gnome

On 14 April 1913 this F.20 was in the RAF, designated as a No. 3 Squadron aircraft. It did much flying with that unit, including artillery observation in July 1913, and was later modified to have a Vickers gun installed in the forward cockpit and the pilot moved to the rear. Although on the strength of 'C' Flight, No. 3 Squadron, on 31 July 1914, it did not go to France. It crashed on 13 August and was struck off on 31 August. (RAF Museum)

286 HENRY FARMAN F.20
80hp Gnome

No. 286 was awaited by No. 3 Squadron at the end of April 1913 and had been taken on strength by 9 May. Ten days later it was used by Lt. G. I. Carmichael and Capt. D. G. Conner in experiments with Very signal-pistol lights. Thereafter it regular pilot was Lt. N. S. Roupell, who on 27 August flew in it to help Lt. R. Cholmondeley, who had crashed No. 274 at Dorton. Unfortunately Roupell also crashed while trying to take off at Dorton. The remains of No. 286 were taken back to Netheravon, but the Farman was not rebuilt. (RAF Museum)

287 GRAHAME-WHITE TYPE VIII
60hp Anzani

An unconfirmed process of elimination suggests that the Grahame-White Type VIII was the likeliest recipient of the number 287. It was exhibited at the 1913 Olympia Aero Show as a seaplane, but later flew at Hendon with a wheel undercarriage of bizarre complexity. Bought by the War Office in April 1913, it was damaged at Farnborough, as seen here. Apparently No. 287 was not flown by the RFC until October, perhaps after repair, and, although tested the next month, it was struck off on 26 November 1913. (RAF Museum)

288 AVRO TYPE Es/502
50hp Gnome

This Avro Type Es was reported to be flying with No. 3 Squadron on 25 June 1913. Its most frequent pilot was Lt. E. L. Conran, but it was also flown by Maj. H.R.M. Brooke-Popham and Lts. V.H.N. Wadham and P.B. Joubert de la Ferté. By January 1914 it was with No. 5 Squadron, and in September it was with 'A' Flight at CFS, with ailerons in place of wing warping. (JMB/GSL)

289 AVRO TYPE Es/502
50hp Gnome

The history of No. 289 resembles that of No. 288. It was with No. 3 Squadron by 19 June 1913; in addition to being flown by Lts. Joubert and Wadham, its pilots included Lts. J. E. G. Burroughs and T. W. Mulcahy-Morgan and Maj. G. H. Raleigh. It, too, went to No. 5 Squadron, and was an aircraft of 'A' Flight CFS in September 1914. (JMB/GSL)

290 AVRO TYPE Es/502
50hp Gnome

Taken on charge on 6 June 1913, this aeroplane was with No. 3 Squadron by 1 July, when it was flown by Lt. Joubert. Its other pilots included Maj. Brooke-Popham, Capt. W. Picton-Warlow, Lts. Burroughs, Wadham, W. C. K. Birch and A. E. Morgan, and Sgts. W. R. Bruce, W. T. J. McCudden and F. Ridd. It was also with No. 5 Squadron at one time. (JMB/GSL)

291 AVRO TYPE Es/502
50hp Gnome

Last of the five Avro Type Es
single-seaters supplied to the
Military Wing, No. 291 was used
first by No. 3 Squadron, later by
No. 5, and was overhauled and
modified with ailerons replacing
the original wing-warping lateral
control. It was at the CFS in
October 1914. (JMB/GSL)

293 BLÉRIOT XI
50hp Gnome

On 26 August 1913 Lt. P. B. Joubert
de la Ferté flew this single-seat,
50hp Blériot XI from Farnborough
to No. 3 Squadron at Netheravon.
He was its regular pilot, in
particular during the manoeuvres
of September 1913, and at least
until 23 October. No. 293 was
tested to destruction at the RAF on
6 November 1913, possibly in
connection with the Military Wing
ban on monoplanes. The
photograph at far right shows No.
293 with No. 292 at Wantage in
September 1913, while the aircraft
were on their way to participate in
the Army Manoeuvres. (JMB/GSL;
P. F. G. Wright)

292 BLÉRIOT XI-2
80hp Gnome

This two-seat Blériot was with No. 3 Squadron by September 1913, when it was flown in that month's Army Manoeuvres. It was one of a few Military Wing aircraft that saw brief use at the Naval Aviation School, Eastchurch, where it arrived on 6 November 1913. By 31 July 1914 it was in 'A' Flight, No. 3 Squadron, and went to France on 13 August. It was wrecked on 10 September 1914. (JMB/GSL)

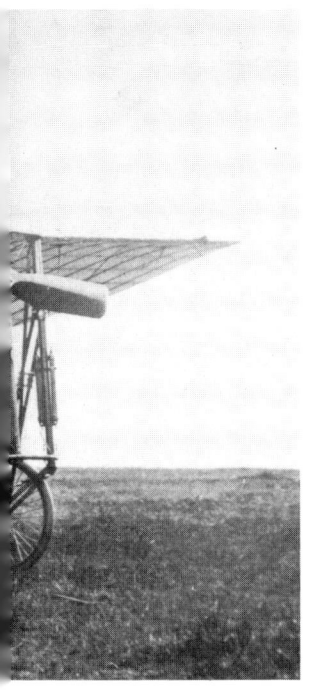

294 HENRY FARMAN F.20
80hp Gnome

This F.20 was with No. 3 Squadron by 23 October 1913, and was on the strength of 'C' Flight of that unit on 31 July 1914. It did not reach France, however, and was reported to have crashed at Shoreham on 14 August. After repair it lasted at least until 22 February 1916, when it was flown by Sgt. (later Major) J. T. B. McCudden. At that time it may have been with No. 1 Reserve Aeroplane Squadron. The photograph shows the aircraft at Shoreham with Lt. E. L. Conran aboard. (Philip M. Jarrett)

300 SOPWITH D.1
80hp Gnome

The recommendation that nine of these Sopwith biplanes be purchased for the Military Wing was made on 5 July 1913; the first was being tested early in November, and the last was delivered to Farnborough on 20 January 1914. No. 300, here seen flying at Farnborough, possibly in April 1914, must have been delivered in December 1913; it was used by No. 5 Squadron and was apparently struck off in August 1914. (PRO:AIR 1/728/176/3/38)

304 CODY BIPLANE
120hp Austro-Daimler

The Military Wing's second Cody was taken on charge by No. 4 Squadron on 20 February 1913 but was wrecked during March. By 3 April it was in Cody's sheds at Farnborough awaiting a decision on repair. Possibly the fatal crash of No. 301 caused No. 304 to be abandoned, but it was not destroyed, and it was decided in November that it should be presented to the Science Museum, where it now resides. (JMB/GSL)

301 CODY BIPLANE
Ex-Military Trials No. 31, 120hp Austro-Daimler

Winner of the Military Aeroplane Competition that ended on 27 August 1912, the Cody was not officially taken on charge until 27 November, and was handed to No. 4 Squadron shortly before Christmas. Cody was allowed to exhibit it at Olympia in February 1913, and he was instructing Lt. L. C. Rogers-Harrison on it on 24 February. Although re-wired in mid-April, the aeroplane broke up in the air on 28 April, Rogers-Harrison losing his life. The number 301 was later re-allocated to a Maurice Farman S.7. (JMB/GSL)

305 MAURICE FARMAN S.7
70hp Renault

Flown from Hendon by Pierre Verrier on delivery to Farnborough on 24 February 1913 and tested on 26 February, this aircraft was taken on charge by No. 4 Squadron on 11 March. Its flying career was undistinguished, its pilots including Maj. Raleigh, Capts. Board and Reynolds, and Lts. Atkinson, Chinnery, Gould, Holt and Unwin. By 19 December its flying time totalled 123hrs 19mins, and when struck off on 11 June 1914 the total was 155hrs 9mins. (K. M. Molson)

307 MAURICE FARMAN S.7
70hp Renault

This Longhorn was delivered to Farnborough by air on 25 March 1913, was handed over to the Military Wing on 11 April and was officially taken on charge the next day. By 21 April it was with No. 4 Squadron, and did much flying. It went to Netheravon on 19 June when the unit moved there, flying regularly thereafter at least until August 1913. On 27 July 1914 it went to the Aircraft Manufacturing Co. for reconstruction, and in September was with No. 1 Squadron.

309 GRAHAME-WHITE BIPLANE
50hp Gnome

No. 309 was allotted to a 'Henry Farman type' fitted with a 50hp Gnome, one of the eight or nine assorted aircraft reportedly bought from Grahame-White in March and April 1913 to bring the Military Wing's strength up to the numbers claimed by Col. Seely. This primitive biplane is, *prima facie*, the only one of the group to fit that description, yet its implied destination, No. 4 Squadron, seems unlikely. The aircraft illustrated must have been the former No. 5 of the Grahame-White flying school, first flown on 9 March 1912. Apparently No. 309 flew for only ten minutes in the RFC. (JMB/GSL)

311 CAUDRON BIPLANE
45hp Anzani

Built by Hewlett & Blondeau for the W. H. Ewen Aviation Co. Ltd., this small Caudron was acquired by the War Office in May 1913. It was with No. 4 Squadron by 11 September, when it was approvingly flown by Lt. G. I. Carmichael. Further flights were made, to no great purpose, in October and November, and by 19 December its flying time totalled 17hrs 27mins. The aircraft could not be regarded as effective, and it was struck off in April 1914. (JMB/GSL)

315 SOPWITH D.1
80hp Gnome

Records of the service of the Sopwith tractors in No. 5 Squadron are disappointingly scanty, but the squadron's seeming unwillingness to take any of them to France in August 1914 suggests that they were not highly regarded. This photograph (date and locale unknown) leaves no doubt that No. 315 was involved in at least one accident. (JMB/GSL)

319 SOPWITH D.1
80hp Gnome

In June 1914 two Sopwiths of this type were present at the RFC Concentration Camp at Netheravon, where this photograph was taken. No. 319 was an aircraft of No. 5 Squadron, probably one of the four that the squadron had mustered in its practice mobilization on 22 April 1914. Following a crash in July, the aircraft was struck off on 21 August 1914. (Bruce Robertson)

323 BLÉRIOT XI
50hp Gnome

Apparently taken on charge in February 1914, this single-seat Blériot had an obscure career. For a time it was on the strength of No. 6 Squadron, and it has been reported that it was detached to Montrose in August 1914. The following month it was with No. 1 Reserve Aeroplane Squadron at Farnborough. (Crown Copyright, RAE)

324, 325 SOPWITH D.1
80hp Gnome

These two Sopwiths of No. 5 Squadron collided in flight on 12 May 1914 and, as the photographs show, were completely destroyed. The only survivor of the disaster was Lt. C. W. Wilson, the pilot of No. 325; the occupants of No. 324, Capt. E. V. Anderson and AM Carter, were killed. (JMB/GSL; JMB/GSL)

326 SOPWITH S.S.1 TABLOID
80hp Gnome

Due for delivery on 9 March 1914 but not delivered until 13 May, No. 326 was allocated to No. 5 Squadron but apparently did little or no flying pending the provision of a strengthened undercarriage. It was at Farnborough early in July, but did not go to France. Following a brief association with No. 1 Squadron, the aeroplane was transferred to the Central Flying School on 8 December 1914. (Crown Copyright, RAE)

328 ROYAL AIRCRAFT FACTORY B.E.2a
70hp Renault

The airborne B.E.2a in this photograph taken at Montrose is No. 328, which had initially been numbered 461. It was handed over from the CFS to the Military Wing on 26 January 1914 and was taken on charge by No. 2 Squadron on 18 April. On 19 May it left Montrose with the Netheravon Concentration Camp as its ultimate destination. It crashed on 25 July and was struck off charge. (JMB/GSL)

331 ROYAL AIRCRAFT FACTORY B.E.2a
70hp Renault

This B.E.2a, here seen at Farnborough in a photograph dated 10 February 1914, was assigned to the Military Wing on 21 April that year and was flown from Farnborough to No. 2 Squadron at Montrose by Lt. J. Empson. On 15 May he left Montrose for York, en route to Netheravon and the Concentration Camp, but crashed on landing. Both Lt. Empson and his passenger, AM Cudmore, were killed. The B.E. was struck off on 3 July. (Crown Copyright, RAE)

114

336 ROYAL AIRCRAFT FACTORY B.E.2a
70hp Renault

Built by Vickers, this B.E.2a was delivered to Farnborough on 29 January 1914 and was fitted with wireless. On 31 July it was earmarked for No. 4 Squadron, with which unit it went to France on 13 August, but it was transferred on 5 October to HQ Wireless Squadron, which became No. 9 Squadron on 4 December. It went to the Aircraft Park on 25 January 1915, was issued to No. 2 Squadron on 4 March, and went to No. 4 Squadron (via the AP) on 1 August. Its last operational allocation was to No. 8 Squadron on 11 August; it returned to England on 10 October 1915 and subsequently went to the CFS. (JMB/GSL)

343 MAURICE FARMAN S.11
70hp Renault

Originally numbered 464, this Shorthorn exchanged identities with a Longhorn and was taken on charge by the Military Wing on 20 May 1914. It saw brief service with No. 6 Squadron during that unit's working-up period, and continued in a training capacity with No. 1 Reserve Aeroplane Squadron at Farnborough. In December 1914 it went briefly to Lydd for Home Defence duties. (JMB/GSL)

347 ROYAL AIRCRAFT FACTORY B.E.2a
70hp Renault

Built by Coventry Ordnance Works and due for delivery on 29 July 1913, this B.E.2a was eventually delivered on 26 February 1914. Although in 'A' Flight of No. 2 Squadron on 31 July, it did not go to France: the next day it was under repair in the RAF. It saw some training service with No. 1 Reserve Aeroplane Squadron at Farnborough, and by January 1915 was at the CFS. (*Flight International*)

351 HENRY FARMAN F.20
80hp Gnome

Taken on charge on 18 April 1913, No. 351 went to No. 3 Squadron at Netheravon and was frequently flown, mostly by Capt. P.L.W. Herbert and Lt. D. L. Allen. After lengthy overhaul (6 January–27 April 1914) it returned to No. 3 Squadron on 28 May and went to France in 'C' Flight on 13 August. It went to the Aircraft Park on 20 November, was re-issued to No. 5 Squadron on 12 December, but was wrecked six days later. (JMB/GSL)

352 HENRY FARMAN F.20
80hp Gnome

By 7 July 1913 this Farman was with No. 3 Squadron, having first been taken on charge on 24 April. Its regular pilots were Lts. T. O'Brien Hubbard and R. Cholmondeley, and it was used in early experiments with a Vickers gun, its nacelle being modified to transpose the positions of pilot and observer. No. 3 Squadron took the aircraft to France on 13 August 1914, and it was wrecked there on 12 September. (JMB/GSL)

354 GRAHAME-WHITE TYPE VIIc
70hp Gnome

Another of the motley collection of aircraft hastily purchased from Grahame-White in the spring of 1913, this biplane had appeared in mid-November 1912 and was wordily catalogued as the Grahame-White Popular Passenger Biplane Type VIIc. It was taken on Military Wing charge on 20 April 1913, but apparently was never serviceable, never went to a squadron, and was struck off charge on 20 December 1913. (JMB/GSL)

355 MAURICE FARMAN S.7
70hp Renault

The RFC took No. 355 on charge on 17 May 1913, and it flew at Farnborough with the Flying Depot before going to No. 5 Squadron. It is believed to have been with that unit between August 1913 and April 1914. Allocation to No. 7 Squadron was proposed but probably not implemented, for the aircraft was struck off charge on 22 May 1914. (RAF Museum)

362 ROYAL AIRCRAFT FACTORY R.E.1
No. 2, 70hp Renault

The number 362 was allocated to three different aircraft: a COW-built B.E.2a that was renumbered 474; the second R.E.1 (from 6 to 10 March 1914), which probably never shed its original number, 608; and a Sopwith Tabloid. At the material time the R.E.1 was officially on charge with the Military Wing, the Tabloid not being taken on charge until 7 August 1914. (JMB/GSL)

365 ROYAL AIRCRAFT FACTORY B.E.8
80hp Gnome

Two B.E.8s were ordered from the British & Colonial Aeroplane Co. under Contract No. A/2238 dated 18 August 1913. The first of these aircraft, No. 365, was due for delivery on 8 January 1914 and was delivered to Farnborough on 10 March. It was not allocated to any squadron, but was subjected to static loading tests in the Royal Aircraft Factory. This photograph of No. 365 under test bears the date 24 June 1914. (Crown Copyright, RAE)

366 DUNNE D.8
80hp Gnome

The contract under which this aircraft was ordered was dated 19 March 1913 and called for its delivery on 14 May 1913. It was in fact delivered on 3 March 1914, although it had apparently been completed by early October 1913. The RFC's Dunne was flying at Farnborough on 11 March 1914, but it seemed that the Military Wing did not know what to do with the aircraft. It was still at Farnborough, dismantled, in August 1914. (Crown Copyright, RAE)

369 MAURICE FARMAN S.11
70hp Renault

Taken on charge on 28 May 1914, this early Shorthorn saw brief service with No. 6 Squadron and with No. 1 Reserve Aeroplane Squadron before going to Egypt in November 1914. It probably was the solitary Shorthorn that was with No. 30 Squadron from May 1915 until withdrawn for reconstruction in February 1916, and it is seen here with an anonymous B.E.2b that was used by 'C' Flight of No. 30 Squadron at Ismailia. (RAF Museum)

372 ROYAL AIRCRAFT FACTORY B.E.2a
70hp Renault

Vickers-built, and due for delivery on 9 January 1914, this B.E.2a was delivered on 23 March. It was flown by Hereward de Havilland on 23 May, and went to France in 'C' Flight of No. 2 Squadron on 13 August. There it was struck off charge on 28 August 1914. (JMB/GSL)

373 ROYAL AIRCRAFT FACTORY B.E.8
80hp Gnome

The second of the two B.E.8s ordered from British & Colonial under Contract No. A/2238, No. 373 was due to be delivered on 22 January 1914 and was in fact delivered on 28 March. Somewhat tentatively associated with No. 7 Squadron, it was on 31 July 1914 earmarked for No. 5 Squadron but did not cross the Channel until 8 October, when No. 6 Squadron took it to Belgium. It was wrecked on 17 October 1914. (Crown Copyright, RAE)

374, 375 BLÉRIOT XI-2
80hp Gnome

Both ordered under Contract A/2354 of 28 January 1914, both due for delivery on 28 February and both delivered on 31 March, these two Blériot two-seaters saw relatively little service. They were allocated to No. 3 Squadron, No. 374 on 22 April and its companion a day earlier, but both aircraft were damaged on 30 June 1914. No. 375 was struck off charge on 17 July 1914. (JMB/GSL)

376 AVRO 504
80hp Gnome

The first of twelve Avro 504s ordered under Contract A/2367 of 1 April 1914, No. 376 was due for delivery on 29 April but was not delivered until 12 June. It was reported to have flown on 18 May, but on arrival at Farnborough was tested to destruction, as seen in this photograph dated (probably belatedly) 8 September 1914. The number 376 was also allotted to a Vickers-built B.E.2a that was delivered on 16 June but renumbered 475. (Crown Copyright, RAE)

378 SOPWITH S.S.1 TABLOID
80hp Gnome

Of the initial batch of nine S.S.1 Tabloids ordered under Contract A/2368 of 18 December 1913, the first was due to be delivered on 27 February 1914, but it is seen here at Brooklands shortly before its actual delivery flight to Farnborough on 22 April. One official document indicates that it was damaged on arrival; certainly it was tested to destruction in the RAF, as seen in the second photograph (which is dated 15 June 1914). (Crown Copyright, RAE)

379 MAURICE FARMAN S.11
70hp Renault

This Shorthorn was taken on charge on 5 April 1914 and has been reported as an aircraft of No. 4 Squadron, and subsequently of the CFS. By June 1915 it was with No. 1 Reserve Aeroplane Squadron, Farnborough, and was still there on 14 December 1915. On 18 May 1916 it was in the Reserve Aircraft Park at Farnborough, assigned to the 6th Brigade and evidently intended for further training duties. (JMB/GSL)

380 ROYAL AIRCRAFT FACTORY R.E.5
No. 6, 120hp Austro-Daimler

This R.E.5, the sixth of 24 ordered, was delivered on 28 April 1914 and went to No. 6 Squadron. On 15 and 16 June 1914 Maj. J. H. W. Becke made two unsuccessful attempts to break the altitude record of 18,900ft set on a similar long-span R.E.5 by Norman Spratt on 14 May. No. 380 went to the Aircraft Park in France on 28 September and was allocated to No. 2 Squadron on 1 November. It was wrecked on 14 December. (JMB/GSL)

382 ROYAL AIRCRAFT FACTORY R.E.5
No. 10, 120hp Austro-Daimler

No. 382 was an equal-span R.E.5 that was delivered on 13 May 1914. It went to No. 6 Squadron, but engine unserviceability kept it grounded and it was returned to the RAF, where it was inspected after reconstruction on 26 March 1915. It was an aircraft of 'C' Flight at the CFS in March 1916. (Crown Copyright, RAE)

383 ROYAL AIRCRAFT FACTORY B.E.2a
70hp Renault

Here seen in the Armstrong Whitworth works at Gosforth, this was the first of two B.E.2as ordered under Contract No. A/2356 of 13 January 1914. It was due for delivery on 7 May, was actually delivered on 20 May, and was taken on charge by the Military Wing on 6 August. It went to France with No. 2 Squadron on 13 August, was returned to the 1st Aircraft Park on 11 May 1915, and was struck off charge on 29 May 1915. (JMB/GSL)

394 SOPWITH S.S.1 TABLOID
80hp Gnome

Almost certainly the Tabloid flown to Farnborough by Harry Hawker on 29 June 1914, No. 394 was taken on charge by the Military Wing on 28 July; it went first to No. 7 Squadron and possibly then to No. 6. This photograph, taken at Farnborough, is dated 18 August. The aeroplane was one of three Tabloids sold to the RNAS by the Military Wing on 9 September: renumbered fleetingly 904, and finally 167, it was the Tabloid flown by Lt. Cdr. Spenser Grey on the attempted bombing raid on the Cologne airship sheds on 8 October 1914 (see page 68). Abandoned at Antwerp, it was deleted on 14 October. (Crown Copyright, RAE)

398 AVRO 504
80hp Gnome

The Farnborough photograph (top) is dated 29 July 1914, and No. 398 was taken on charge on 11 August. It went to France with No. 5 Squadron on 15 August, and the second photograph is of this Avro in service with that squadron in the spring of 1915, with its serial number presented in smaller characters (perhaps necessitated by the painting of a roundel on the rudder). No. 398 was sent to the 1st Aircraft Park on 17 June 1915, and although recorded as under reconstruction at 31 July it did not reappear in subsequent records of the RFC in France. (Crown Copyright, RAE; R. Vann)

Aircraft Nos. 1–400

Aircraft shown in **bold type** are illustrated in this book

1   (i) **Short Pusher Biplane, S.34**; (ii) **Short Type S.38 Pusher Biplane, S.86.**
2   (i) **Short Pusher Biplane, S.38**; (ii) **S.38 rebuilt.**
3   (i) **Short Triple-Twin Biplane, S.39**; (ii) **Short Pusher Biplane, S.78.** See also No. 181.
4   **Short Triple-Tractor Biplane, S.47.**
5   **Short Tractor Biplane, S.45.**
6   Breguet C2/U2 Biplane.
7   **Deperdussin Monoplane.**
8   **Short Monoplane, S.42.**
9   **Etrich Monoplane.**
10 **Short Tractor Biplane, S.41.** See also No. 180.
11 **Henry Farman Seaplane.**
12 Short Twin-Engined Monoplane, S.46.
13 Nieuport IV.G Monoplane. Renumbered 409.
14 Short Four-Seat Seaplane, 2× 140hp Gnome. Not delivered.
15 Bristol T.B.8.
16 **Avro 501.**
17 **RAF H.R.E.2.**
18 **Donnet-Lévêque Flying Boat.**
19 **Short Tractor Seaplane, S.54.**
20 **Short Tractor Seaplane, S.57.**
21 Short Tractor Seaplane, S.56.
22 Deperdussin Monoplane, 80hp Anzani.
23 Maurice Farman S.7.
24 Bristol Boxkite.
25 Astra Seaplane, 100hp Renault. Not delivered.
26 (i) **RAF H.R.E.3**; (ii) **RAF R.E.5 No.14.**
27 (i) **Sopwith School Biplane**; (ii) Rebuilt as **Sopwith D.1.**
28 **Short Type S.38 Pusher Biplane, S.55.**
29 **Maurice Farman Seaplane.**
30 (i) Royal Aircraft Factory Two-Seat Seaplane (not delivered); (ii) Deperdussin Monoplane Seaplane, 100hp Anzani.
31 Henry Farman Biplane.
32 **Vickers F.B.5.**
33 Sopwith D.1.
34 **Short Type S.38 Pusher Biplane, S.61.**
35 Bristol Boxkite.
36 Deperdussin Monoplane, 80hp Anzani.
37 Borel Monoplane Seaplane.
38 **Sopwith Bat-Boat.**
39 Blériot XI-2.
40 Caudron G.3.
41 Avro Type E.

42 **Short Tractor Seaplane, S.60.**
43 **Bristol T.B.8.**
44 Deperdussin Seaplane, 100hp Anzani.
45 Caudron G.3.
46 (i) **RAF B.E.2a**; (ii) RAF B.E.2c.
47 (i) RAF B.E.2a; (ii) **RAF B.E.2c.**
48 **Borel Monoplane Seaplane.**
49 RAF B.E.2a.
50 RAF B.E.2a.
51 Avro 503.
52 Avro 503.
53 Avro 503.
54 Coventry Ordnance Works seaplane. Not delivered.
55 **Caudron Amphibian.**
56 **Caudron Amphibian.**
57 **Caudron Amphibian.**
58 **Sopwith HT.**
59 **Sopwith HT.**
60 **Sopwith HT.**
61 Sopwith Hydro Biplane Type S, 2× 120hp Austro-Daimler. Built but not accepted.
62 **Short Type S.38 Pusher Biplane, S.66.**
63 Short Type S.38 Pusher Biplane, S.67.
64 Short Type S.38 Pusher Biplane, S.76.
65 **Short Type S.38 Pusher Biplane, S.75.**
66 **Short Type S.38 Pusher Biplane, S.77.**
67 **Maurice Farman S.7.**
68 RAF H.R.E.6. Not built.
69 **Maurice Farman S.7.**
70 **Maurice Farman S.7.**
71 Maurice Farman Seaplane, 70hp Renault.
72 Maurice Farman Seaplane, 70hp Renault.
73 **Maurice Farman Seaplane.**
74 **Short Seaplane, Admiralty Type 74, S.69.**
75 **Short Seaplane, Admiralty Type 74, S.70.**
76 **Short Seaplane, Admiralty Type 74, S.71.**
77 **Short Seaplane, Admiralty Type 74, S.72.**
78 **Short Tractor Seaplane, S.73.**
79 **Short Tractor Seaplane, S.74.**
80 **Short Pusher Seaplane, S.79.**
81 **Short Folder Seaplane, S.64.**
82 **Short Folder Seaplane, S.65.**
83 **Borel Monoplane Seaplane.**
84 **Borel Monoplane Seaplane.**
85 **Borel Monoplane Seaplane.**

86 **Borel Monoplane Seaplane.**
87 Borel Monoplane Seaplane.
88 **Borel Monoplane Seaplane.**
89, 90 Short aircraft, Contract C.P.34603/13. Cancelled.
91, 92 Maurice Farman aircraft, Contract No. C.P.01720/13 with Aircraft Manufacturing Co. Cancelled.
93 Sopwith Gun-Carrying Seaplane, 200hp Salmson.
94 Avro 509 Gun-Carrying Seaplane, 2× 120hp Austro-Daimler. Not delivered.
95 **Maurice Farman Seaplane.**
96 **Henry Farman Seaplane.**
97 **Henry Farman Seaplane.**
98 **Henry Farman Seaplane.**
99 Henry Farman Seaplane.
100 Henry Farman Seaplane.
101 'Blank number' in official list.
102 Henry Farman Seaplane.
103 **Sopwith D.1.**
104 **Sopwith D.1.**
105 **Hamble River, Luke & Co. H.L.1.**
106, 107 Astra Seaplanes. Completion unlikely.
108 Henry Farman Biplane. Completion unlikely.
109 Maurice Farman Biplane. Completion unlikely.
110 Breguet Seaplane, 200hp Salmson.*
111, 112 Breguet Seaplanes, 200hp Salmson. Not delivered.
113 **Maurice Farman Seaplane.**
114 **Maurice Farman Seaplane.**
115 **Maurice Farman Seaplane.**
116 Maurice Farman Seaplane, 120hp Renault.
117 **Maurice Farman Seaplane.**
118 **Sopwith Bat-Boat.**
119 **Short Folder Seaplane, S.82.**
120 **Short Folder Seaplane, S.83.**
121 **Short Folder Seaplane, S.84.**
122 **Short Folder Seaplane, S.85.**
123 **Sopwith Pusher Seaplane.**
124 **Sopwith Pusher Seaplane.**
125 Farman Gun-Carrying Seaplane. On order in February 1914 but apparently not delivered.
126 **Short Gun-Carrying Seaplane, S.81.**
127 **Sopwith Bat-Boat.**
128 **Wight 1914 Navyplane.**
129 **Wight 1914 Navyplane.**
130 **Avro 510.**
131 Avro 510.
132 Avro 510.
133 **Avro 510.**
134 **Avro 510.**
135 Short Folder Seaplane, S.88; 135hp Salmson.

136 **Short Folder Seaplane, S.87.**
137 **Sopwith Tractor Seaplane.**
138 **Sopwith Tractor Seaplane.**
139 **Henry Farman Seaplane.**
140 **Henry Farman Seaplane.**
141 **Henry Farman Seaplane.**
142 **Henry Farman Seaplane.**
143 **Henry Farman Seaplane.**
144 Henry Farman Seaplane.
145 Single-seat biplane, 65-hp Austro-Daimler. Identification as a Short type seems insecure. Not delivered.
146 **Maurice Farman Pusher Biplane.**
147, 148 Bristol Seaplanes, 200hp Salmson. Cancelled.
149 **Sopwith Two-Seater.**
150 **Avro Type E.**
151 **Sopwith Tractor Seaplane.**
152 Short Type S.38, 'sociable' version, S.89; 80hp Gnome.
153 **Bristol T.B.8.**
154 **D.F.W. Military Arrow Biplane.**
155 Wight 1914 Navyplane, 200hp Salmson.
156 Henry Farman Seaplane, 80hp Gnome.
157 Sopwith Type C Tractor Seaplane, 200hp Salmson.
158 Sopwith Type C Tractor Seaplane, 200hp Salmson.
159 Sopwith Type C Tractor Seaplane, 200hp Salmson.
160 Sopwith Single-Seat Biplane, 80hp Gnome Monosoupape. Apparently not delivered.
161 **Short Type C Tractor Seaplane, S.90.**
162 **Short Type C Tractor Seaplane, S.91.**
163 **Short Type C Tractor Seaplane, S.92.**
164 Short Type C Tractor Seaplane, S.93.
165 **Short Type C Tractor Seaplane, S.94.**
166 **Short Type C Tractor Seaplane, S.95.**

---

*Officially listed as a Breguet seaplane, but a report in *The Aeroplane* of 9 April 1914 states that a Henry Farman seaplane No. 110 overturned on 1 April 1914. This could be mistaken, either as to identity or correct number. No seaplanes of any type numbered 110–112 appear in the official lists of February or July 1914. An unidentified Breguet seaplane 'on order for the Government' was at Brighton in July 1913 and was first flown by Henri Brégi on 25 July. It was damaged on 6 August but was apparently at Calshot early in October. Probably not accepted.

167 **Sopwith S.S.1 Tabloid.** Ex-RFC 394.

168 **Sopwith S.S.1 Tabloid.** Ex-RFC 395.

169 **Sopwith Tabloid prototype.** Ex-RFC 604.

170 **Sopwith Special Seaplane.**

171 Wight A.I. Improved Navyplane.

172 **Wight A.I. Improved Navyplane.**

173 Wight A.I. Improved Navyplane.

174 **Wight A.I. Improved Navyplane.**

175 Wight A.I. Improved Navyplane.

176 **Wight A.I. Improved Navyplane.**

177 Wight A.I. Improved Navyplane.

178 Short Two-Seat Biplane, 200hp Salmson. Apparently not built.

179 **Avro 504.**

180 Listed as 'Short 10'; two-seat biplane for 100hp Gnome. No known record of delivery; possibly intended for renumbering of No. 10, Short S.41, but not used.

181 Listed as 'Short 3'; two-seat biplane for 50hp Gnome. No known record of delivery; possibly intended for renumbering of No. 3, Short S.78, but not used.

182 Short Seaplane, 100hp Gnome, possibly a dual-control version of Admiralty Type 74; apparently not built.

183 **Short Seaplane, Admiralty Improved Type 74, S.128.**

184 **Short Seaplane, Admiralty Type 184, S.106.**

185 **Short Seaplane, Admiralty Type 184, S.107.**

186 Short Torpedo-Carrying Seaplane, 2×200hp Salmson. Not built.

187 **Wight Twin Seaplane.**

188 Maurice Farman Biplane, 70hp Renault.

189 Hénry Farman Biplane, 70hp Gnome.

190–198 Short Two-Seat Biplanes, 200hp Salmson. None delivered.

199 Royal Aircraft Factory Seaplane. One official list indicates construction by Short Brothers, but the aircraft was not delivered.

200 **Spencer Biplane.**

201 **RAF B.E.1.**

202 **Breguet L1/U1.**

203 **RAF B.E.3.**

204 **RAF B.E.4.**

205 **RAF B.E.2a.**

206 **RAF B.E.2a.**

207 **Maurice Farman S.7.**

208 Henry Farman Pusher Biplane. Renumbered 412.

209 **Henry Farman Pusher Biplane.** Renumbered 420.

210 **Breguet G3.**

211 **Breguet G3.**

212 **Breguet L2/U1.**

213 **Breguet L2.**

214 **Maurice Farman S.7.**

215 **Maurice Farman S.7.**

216 **Maurice Farman S.7.**

217 **RAF B.E.2a.**

218 **RAF B.E.2a.**

219 **Blériot XI.**

220 **RAF B.E.2a.**

221 **Blériot XI-2.**

222 RAF B.E.2a.

223 Maurice Farman S.7.

224 **Maurice Farman S.7.**

225 **RAF B.E.2a.**

226 **RAF B.E.2a.**

227 **RAF B.E.2a.**

228 **RAF B.E.2a.**

229 **RAF B.E.2a.**

230 RAF B.E.2a.

231 RAF B.E.2a.

232 **RAF B.E.2a.**

233 **RAF B.E.2a.**

234 RAF B.E.2a.

235 **RAF B.E.2a.**

236 RAF B.E.2a.

237 RAF B.E.2a.

238 RAF B.E.2a.

239 **RAF B.E.2a.**

240 **RAF B.E.2a.**

241 RAF B.E.2a.

242 RAF B.E.2a.

243 **Sopwith D.1.**

244 Henry Farman F.20.

245 RAF B.E.2a.

246 Sopwith D.1.

247 Sopwith D.1.

248 RAF B.E.2a.

249 RAF B.E.2a.

250 RAF B.E.2a.

251 **Blériot XXI.**

252 **Deperdussin Monoplane.**

253 **Nieuport IV.G Monoplane.**

254 **Nieuport IV.G Monoplane.**

255 **Nieuport IV.G Monoplane.**

256 **Bristol-Prier Monoplane.**

257 **Deperdussin Monoplane.**

258 **Deperdussin Monoplane.**

259 Deperdussin Monoplane, 100hp Gnome.

260 (i) **Deperdussin Monoplane**, renumbered 419; (ii) Blériot XI-2.

261 **Bristol-Prier Monoplane.**

262 **Bristol-Coanda Monoplane.**

263 **Bristol-Coanda Monoplane.**

264 Nieuport II.N Single-Seat Monoplane, 28hp Nieuport.

265 **Flanders F.4.**

266 **Maurice Farman S.7.** Possibly renumbered 472.

267 **RAF B.E.2a.**

268 Henry Farman F.20.

269 Maurice Farman S.7.

270 Maurice Farman S.7.

271 (i) RAF B.E.2a; (ii) Blériot XI-2.

272 **RAF B.E.2a.**

273 **RAF B.E.2a.**

274 **Henry Farman F.20.**

275, 276 'Henry Farman type' biplanes; acquired from Grahame-White.

277 **Henry Farman F.20.**

278 **Martin-Handasyde Monoplane.**

279 Deperdussin Two-Seat Monoplane, 70hp Gnome.

280 **Deperdussin Two-Seat Monoplane.**

281 **Flanders F.4.**

282 **Nieuport IV.G Monoplane.**

283 **Grahame-White Type VII.**

284 **Henry Farman F.20.**

285 Avro Type Es.

286 **Henry Farman F.20.**

287 **Grahame-White Type VIII.**

288 **Avro Type Es.**

289 **Avro Type Es.**

290 **Avro Type Es.**

291 **Avro Type Es.**

292 **Blériot XI-2.**

293 **Blériot XI.**

294 **Henry Farman F.20.**

295 Henry Farman F.20.

296 Blériot XI-2.

297 Blériot XI.

298 Blériot XI.

299 RAF B.E.2a.

300 **Sopwith D.1.**

301 (i) **Cody Biplane**; (ii) Maurice Farman S.7.

302 Maurice Farman S.7.

303 RAF B.E.8, 50hp Gnome.

304 **Cody Biplane.**

305 **Maurice Farman S.7.**

306 Maurice Farman S.7.

307 **Maurice Farman S.7.**

308 Caudron Two-Seat Biplane, 45hp Anzani.

309 **Grahame-White Biplane.**

310 Breguet U2.

311 **Caudron Two-Seat Biplane**

312 Breguet U2.

313 Breguet Biplane?

314 RAF B.E.2a.

315 **Sopwith D.1.**

316 RAF B.E.2a.

317 RAF B.E.2a.

318 RAF B.E.2a.

319 **Sopwith D.1.**

320 RAF B.E.2a.

321 RAF B.E.2a.

322 Maurice Farman S.7.

323 **Blériot XI.**

324 **Sopwith D.1.**

325 **Sopwith D.1.**

326 **Sopwith S.S.1. Tabloid.**

327 RAF B.E.2a.

328 **RAF B.E.2a.** Ex-461.

329 RAF B.E.2a.

330 Henry Farman F.20.

331 **RAF B.E.2a.**

332 RAF B.E.2a.

333 Sopwith D.1.

334 RAF R.E.5.

335 RAF R.E.5.

336 **RAF B.E.2a.**

337 Maurice Farman S.7.

338 Maurice Farman S.7.

339 Henry Farman F.20.

340 Henry Farman F.20.

341 Henry Farman F.20.

342 Maurice Farman S.11.

343 **Maurice Farman S.11.** Ex-464.

344 Maurice Farman S.11.

345 Maurice Farman S.11.

346 Henry Farman F.20.

347 **RAF B.E.2a.**

348 RAF B.E.2a.

349 RAF B.E.2a.

350 Henry Farman F.20.

351 **Henry Farman F.20.**

352 **Henry Farman F.20.**

353 Henry Farman F.20.

354 **Grahame-White Type VIIc.**

355 **Maurice Farman S.7.**

356 Maurice Farman S.7.

357 Maurice Farman S.7.

358 Maurice Farman S.7.

359 Maurice Farman S.7.

360 Maurice Farman S.7.

361 RAF R.E.5.

362 (i) **RAF R.E.1**, reverted to 608; (ii) RAF B.E.2a, renumbered 474; (iii) Sopwith S.S.1 Tabloid.

363 Henry Farman F.20.

364 Henry Farman F.20.

365 **RAF B.E.8.**

366 **Dunne D.8.**

367 Henry Farman F.20.

368 RAF B.E.2a.

369 **Maurice Farman S.11.**

370 Maurice Farman S.11.

371 Maurice Farman S.11.

372 **RAF B.E.2a.**

373 **RAF B.E.8.**

374 **Blériot XI-2.**

375 **Blériot XI-2.**

376 (i) **Avro 504**; (ii) RAF B.E.2a, renumbered 475.

377 RAF B.E.8.

378 **Sopwith S.S.1 Tabloid.**

379 **Maurice Farman S.11.** .

380 **RAF R.E.5.**

381 Sopwith S.S.1 Tabloid.

382 **RAF R.E.5.**

383 **RAF B.E.2a.**

384 RAF B.E.2a.

385 RAF B.E.2a.

386 Sopwith S.S.1 Tabloid.

387 Sopwith S.S.1 Tabloid.

388 **Blériot XI-2.**

389 Blériot XI-2.

390 Avro 504.

391 RAF B.E.8.

392 Sopwith S.S.1. Tabloid.

393 Henry Farman F.20.

394 **Sopwith S.S.1. Tabloid.** Renumbered 904, then 167.

395 Sopwith S.S.1. Tabloid. Renumbered 905, then 168.

396 RAF B.E.2b.

397 Avro 504.

398 **Avro 504.**

399 RAF B.E.8.

400 No known allocation.